TO LIFE!

Rediscovering Biblical Church

Steve Maltz

**SAFFRON
PLANET**

Saffron Planet

PO Box 2215

Ilford IG1 9TR

UK

T: +44 (0) 208 551 1719

E: contact@saffronplanet.net

ISBN 978-0-9562296-1-8

Typeset by documen, www.documen.co.uk

Cover design by Phil Maltz

Printed in the United Kingdom

*"Do not trust the horse, Trojans. Whatever it is,
I fear the Greeks, even though they bring gifts."*
Virgil, Aeneid

*See to it that no-one takes you captive through
hollow and deceptive philosophy, which depends
on human tradition and the basic principles of this
world rather than on Christ.* (Colossians 2:8)

*Thanks again to the usual suspects, particularly
Kit, Chris, Beresford, Jackie, Kevin and Mark, but
especially to my fantastic wife Monica, my fiercest
and gentlest critic.*

Dedicated to the memory of

Steve Acott (1954-2010)

Mike Flanagan (1955-2010)

Missed and not forgotten

Contents

Introduction

This is the book I've always wanted to read, let alone write! Ever since I became a Christian in August 1987 and joined the narrow path that lay beyond the old rugged cross, it's what lay beyond those simple certainties that soon troubled me.

The path widened alarmingly and I discovered that behind the facade of smiling, earnest faces, there was a World of disunity, confusion, strife and factionalism. Becoming a believer in the risen Christ pulls you into a multi-faceted community, but it's not a comfortable one. You are told that you have joined a worldwide family of believers in the Way, the Truth and the Life, but you are not told of the many different ways and truths and lives!

Most take the safe route of familiarity, living out their New Life without straying too far from the pool that birthed them. This was never to be my lot. If I am defined by the building where I worship, I have been an Independent Evangelical, a Messianic Jewish believer and a Baptist, though trying not to allow such labels to define me. I have dipped my toe in many waters, some so calm they may as well be dead, some lukewarm, neither here nor there, others positively steaming, spurting hot air all over the place.

Clinging at all times to my identity, my heart welded to Messiah Jesus, I found my mind swayed by tongues, both smooth and forked, convincing me of their particular brand of Christianity. Then there were the questions, so many unanswered questions, even now, twenty four years later.

Why so many "ways"? Why so many varieties of Christianity, the denominations, some soft and forgiving, others hard and exclusive? Why such conflicting "truths", with conflicts over healing, salvation, gifts and worship just for starters? Some are just minor disagreements between friends, others fully-blown battles. How can a people who declare they have the Truth, be so unclear on how this truth is expressed in their thinking and actions? Then there is the "life" of the Christian ...

My goodness, for a people who have been guaranteed a life of purpose in both this World and the World to come, why are we generally seen as miserable, ineffectual, selfish and judgemental? Yes, much of this is negative propaganda from the media, becoming more secular and anti-Christian by the minute, but many of these perceptions are self-inflicted. Where is the true Christian voice in our nation, speaking up to defend our values and beliefs? Ask any non-believer to name a prominent and respected Christian and he would struggle. Then ask him to watch the "God" channels on TV and be surprised if you are not met with bewilderment or even derision. Are Christians meant to be as rich and powerful as these televangelists? If all Christians are granted perfect health and unlimited wealth, as these people seem to be preaching, then why doesn't the World believe, because surely that's what we all want in life?

Then there are the other questions I began to ask. Why does God seem to be silent and aloof to some Christians, yet to some others He is a positive chatterbox, sprinkling them with new revelations and mighty words and actions, to say nothing of gold dust and teeth! Why do some folk believe that God has stopped bestowing His gifts on us, no more healings, or prophecy or miracles? Are all these people reading the same Bible? And what about unity? Isn't it our love for our Christian brothers and sisters that marks us out as a special people of God? That's fine when we're dealing with those with whom we agree on those issues that tend to divide. But what of the rest, those with whom we disagree? What does the World really see when they watch how we interact with each other? Do they really see anything that drives them to jealousy and envy, and makes them declare, *I want some of what they have*? Then there are other questions concerning such topics as the rapture, the kingdom, prophets and apostles – all areas where there is so much debate and departure.

Who has got it right? Anyone? Why is it sometimes easier being a Christian in the World than a Christian in the Church? To borrow from the world of theoretical physics, is there a yet-undiscovered "theory of everything" that pulls it all together and brings order out of the ecclesiastical chaos?

I believe there could well be, and this book is my search for it.

PART ONE

The Way

I've Heard of This Church ...

A long time ago, in a far-off place, there was a church; not a building as such, but a group of ordinary people united for an extraordinary purpose. It was the first church in this particular land and, it's fair to say, it made a huge impact there, though only for a relatively short period, as is the way with revivals throughout history.

And what a church it was. Believers met in each other's homes, but were equally at ease on the streets, where people brought their sick to be healed. They also met with the common folk at their own places of worship and debated with them, even winning converts from them. In one instance they converted the leader of such a place and his entire household. Despite some hostility, they preached successfully in the open spaces and the marketplaces. As a result of all this activity, the church grew daily in numbers and in influence, even gaining converts from the priests of the old religion.

Their meetings were times of joy and freedom, an expectation of an encounter and a conversation with God, within the comfort and warmth of a home environment. It was a demonstration of true family; a group comprising of spiritual brothers and sisters communing with their spiritual Father in Heaven. There, with a plentiful supply of food and drink they would fellowship, pray, sing hymns and learn at the feet of the teachers. They would share the memorial meal of bread and wine, reminding them of the body and blood of Messiah Jesus, within a meal patterned on the Passover meal of the Last Supper, but celebrated with decorum demanded by such a solemn occasion. Hence they would ensure that there were no divisions or factions within their group, no hidden niggles and grievances, otherwise they could, in a very real sense, be inviting curses on themselves, rather than the blessing that the Lord's Supper promises.

There were also practical matters to consider at these gatherings of the church. They were to consider themselves fully equal to each other, no hierarchies or favouritism. If any had a particular need then others would freely give support, even if it meant selling their own possessions, including real estate. And this generosity of spirit was also to reach beyond the walls of their meeting places. Funds were collected and sent out to needy brothers and sisters in other churches, even those in other lands, to support the poor, the widows and the orphans. This was not giving from a position of wealth; this was giving, more often than not, from a position of real poverty – everyone gave a proportion of their income, even if their income was tiny. And this was always done with a glad heart.

The church had been planted by a small group of highly-motivated apostles who, in the early days, were the teachers and the preachers and the workers of miracles. And what wonders they performed for the Glory of God, in the name of His son, Jesus Christ; healings, deliverances and the raising of the dead with witnesses to confirm. There were even times when the sick were laid out on mats in the paths of the apostles and it was said that all were healed. On other occasions they would walk from house to house, teaching and preaching and many would be saved or delivered from evil spirits. Many were able to walk for the first time, simply by touch or proclamation. And what was the effect of such an uncommon outburst of God's grace on this land? Before opposition restricted access to this heavenly outpouring, everyone who came in contact with the church was completely filled with awe; it was impossible to remain unaffected. Too much was happening to ignore it, though the existing religious authorities did their best at first, before taking direct action.

Opposition was inevitable, although the church was initially greeted with great favour by the people in the land. Too many religious noses had been put out of joint (those that hadn't been healed!) but these new setbacks were turned into opportunities, allowing great demonstrations of God's power and grace. When one of their number was thrown into prison, the church gathered to pray for him and an angel rescued him. Another time, two apostles were similarly imprisoned and, after witnessing to their fellow prisoners, they were rescued by an earthquake that shattered doors and chains. Their witness was such that their jailer was rescued from a suicide attempt and brought to a dramatic salvation, along with his family. Opposition gave way to persecution and Christian blood was spilled when a charismatic preacher, serving as a deacon, was arrested on a trumped-up charge and killed by the religious leaders, but not before he preached the Gospel to them in power. This martyrdom sparked off an unprecedented missionary effort, taking the revival through lands to the north and the west.

Thus was the story of the first church, the church of Peter, Paul, James and the other friends of Jesus, as described in the Book of the Acts of the Apostles. Of course, what started on that Day of Shavuot (Pentecost), with that first and greatest divine outpouring, was one church, *The Church*, one body of believers, exploding from a handful of disciples to a 3,000+ throng of converts in a single day. That Church, within the lifetime of those first apostles, became a network of *churches*, from Jerusalem to Rome and all points in-between.

What image does that conjure up? If we are honest, the first impression is of a network of buildings, perhaps not the great gothic cathedrals of a later generation, but at least of small, sparse halls, tucked away down some alleyway, identified by, perhaps, a fish symbol on their doorpost. We think *buildings*, because that's how we're conditioned to think, ever since the edicts of Emperor Constantine in the 4th Century AD, when Christianity sold out and became the official State religion.

The actual word, "Church" (and the Scottish derivation, "kirk"), is a curious one, as the Greek word it comes from, *kyriakon*, only appears twice in the New Testament, with the meaning, "belonging to the Lord" (*the Lord's*):

When you come together, it is not the Lord's Supper you eat,
(1 Corinthians 11:20)

On the Lord's Day I was in the Spirit, and I heard behind me a loud voice like a trumpet,
(Revelation 1:10)

This is strange, as in neither case does the word "Church" as we understand it, seem to make sense as a translation. So how has this word been hijacked and why do we find it all over the New Testament translations? We demand an answer!

The Greek word that becomes "Church" throughout these translations is *ekklesia*. There is obviously no etymological (words deriving from other words) connection, as in the Greek word "Christos" becoming *Christ* in English. This suggests that something unusual is going on here, something very human and, perhaps, political. The usual use of *ekklesia* in the Greek world at that time was as an assembly and the actual meaning of the word is "called out". This does give a good sense of how God sees His people.

But you are a chosen people, a royal priesthood, a holy nation, a people belonging to God, that you may declare the praises of him who called you out of darkness into his wonderful light.
(1 Peter 2:9)

Yet we are not called into "ekkleses" but into *churches*. There seems to be a mystery attached to this usage and I will return to this a little later.

So this first church, that of the first apostles, was a "called out" assembly, meeting in private homes, not religious buildings. The Jerusalem church, in its formative years, comprised the early apostles and assorted disciples, male and female, probably meeting in a couple of rooms in the house of (the Gospel writer) Mark's mother.

> *When this had dawned on him, he went to the house of Mary the mother of John, also called Mark, where many people had gathered and were praying.*
> (Acts 12:12)

When numbers got too large they undoubtedly spread out into other homes.

Similarly, the early church in Damascus was probably in the family home of a man called Judas (Acts 9:11), the Thessalonian church could have been birthed in Jason's living room (Acts 17:5) and similarly in Corinth, they could have first met in a spare room at Titius Justus's house (Acts 18:7). We do know that a church met in the house of Aquila and Priscilla (probably in Ephesus).

> *The churches in the province of Asia send you greetings. Aquila and Priscilla greet you warmly in the Lord, and so does the church that meets at their house.*
> (1 Corinthians 16:19)

Again, it's not the usual way we think about such things. We are at the tail end of a history that depicts churches as great old buildings, richly adorned with stained glass windows, rather than the folk who meet therein. These days fewer and fewer people meet in these buildings, apart from those that have become carpet warehouses and nightclubs. And more and more Christian folk are returning to those lost origins, meeting in more familiar, friendly surroundings, which is a most welcome process. So, what does the church do when it meets up? What did the original Church of the apostles do?

As I have already noted, the home was the main meeting place for the church, where they ate together, prayed and worshipped together, met each other's needs, shared bread and wine and testimonies and built each other up as a spiritual family. This theme of *family* is often emphasised in the New Testament accounts of the early Church, though we often miss it through over-familiarity (is there a subtle pun there, not sure?). Note how often the following terms are used, all elements present in family life of the day: brother, sister, father, child, steward, slave, servant.

It was in this environment that these early believers recharged their batteries, performed maintenance tasks and corrected any faults. Straining further at the metaphor, they did all this to ensure a smooth performance and a good report in an outside world that was becoming increasingly challenging and hostile.

In these home churches they would perform many functions very familiar to us today, such as water baptism (sometimes of whole families), laying on of hands (in a sense of focussing attention on an individual) and eating together:

When you come together, it is not the Lord's Supper you eat, for as you eat, each of you goes ahead without waiting for anybody else. One remains hungry, another gets drunk.
(1 Corinthians 11:20-21)

The Greek word used here for "Supper" implies that the Lord's Supper was not just a section of liturgy, grafted into a structured order of service, as we see today. Instead it was an actual meal, just like the *Last Supper*, the Passover meal enjoyed by Jesus and his disciples before his arrest. Surely a re-reading of the verse above makes more sense with Holy Communion being shared as part of an actual meal, doesn't it?

In fact, the act of *breaking bread* does not necessarily refer to the "holy act". At the beginning of a family meal, even with religious Jewish families today, bread is broken as a blessing:

Baruch ata Adonai, Eloheinu Melech ha'olam, hamotzi lechem, min ha aretz: Blessed are You, O LORD our God, King of the Universe, Who has brought forth bread from the earth.

But we mustn't be pedantic about such things, because there is also sufficient evidence for the traditional understanding.

Is not the cup of thanksgiving for which we give thanks a participation in the blood of Christ? And is not the bread that we break a participation in the body of Christ?
(1 Corinthians 10:16)

So, sometimes there is room for alternative explanations. More of this later.

One other thing to mention is something that, in our age of materialism and individualism, has all but disappeared from the Body of Christ, and that is the idea of sharing possessions with each other and supporting each other financially.

All the believers were together and had everything in common. Selling their possessions and goods, they gave to anyone as he had need.
(Acts 2:44-45)

All the believers were one in heart and mind. No one claimed that any of his possessions was his own, but they shared everything they had.
(Acts 4:32)

These days many of us Christians share our houses with our mortgage companies, rather than with each other. This is not an indictment of the modern Church, just a comment on how we in the Western World live our lives today in an age of individualism.

There was another way that Christians helped each other in these house meetings. This was through the exercise of spiritual gifts. We are told that everyone has been supernaturally given at least one gift.

Now to each one the manifestation of the Spirit is given for the common good. To one there is given through the Spirit the message of wisdom, to another the message of knowledge by means of the same Spirit, to another faith by the same Spirit, to another gifts of healing by that one Spirit, to another miraculous powers, to another prophecy, to another distinguishing between spirits, to another speaking in different kinds of tongues, and to still another the interpretation of tongues. All these are the work of one and the same Spirit, and he gives them to each one, just as he determines.

(1 Corinthians 12:7-11)

So everyone who met in these churches had at least one of the following gifts: wisdom, knowledge, faith, healing, miraculous powers, prophecy, discernment, speaking and interpretation of tongues. These gifts were apportioned by the Holy Spirit and they were for the common good, to help other Christians.

How this has changed. The topic of spiritual gifts has become divisive in today's Church. Some ignore them entirely. Some explicitly teach that they are not for today's Church. Some wield them like weapons of self-promotion, as marks of divine favouritism. Where are the modest assemblies, that are truly exercising these gifts in the quiet but powerful way that God intended? They are probably around, but too busy getting on with it to declare their opinions from the rooftops (or Christian TV).

This is a good time to examine how these early Christians organised themselves. What was the management structure? Which Church model did they follow – episcopalian, national, presbyterian or congregational? How did they divide themselves into bishops, archbishops, popes, priests, pastors and all the other offices with which we are familiar?

Well, isn't it amazing what 2,000 years of Church history can produce (though most of this was done within the first couple of centuries)? This is the product of Greek thinking, organising structures and building hierarchies. These early believers, mostly Jewish, preferred the Hebraic model, which "co-incidentally" was also the Biblical Church model.

Those early home churches were just meetings of disciples, believers in the risen Christ. For matters of organisation and discipline, just two offices were created, *elders* and *deacons*, though *apostles* also had their role to play. It was a lot simpler in those days.

So, let us start at the beginning. The apostles. These originally were the twelve men selected by Jesus at the start of his ministry.

These are the names of the twelve apostles: first, Simon (who is called Peter) and his brother Andrew; James son of Zebedee, and his brother John; Philip and Bartholomew; Thomas and Matthew the tax collector; James son of Alphaeus, and Thaddaeus; Simon the Zealot and Judas Iscariot, who betrayed him.
(Matthew 10:2-4)

Then twelve became eleven, after Judas spilled his guts, then back to twelve again with the selection of Matthias by lots. Then Paul saw the risen Jesus and became one. Other apostles included Barnabas (Acts 14:14), Andronicus and Junias (Romans 16:7) and James (Galatians 1:19). Even Jesus himself was called an apostle in Hebrews 3:1.

So there weren't many of them and they seemed to be unusually equipped.

The things that mark an apostle – signs, wonders and miracles – were done among you with great perseverance.
(2 Corinthians 12:12)

They needed to be, because they were the ones chosen – literally *sent out* – to get God's Church started. They needed all the spiritual help they could get and God was to intervene many times to get them out of scrapes and to show His power through their actions. The apostles were involved in teaching, preaching, healing, signs and wonders, deliverances, the planting of individual churches and the appointment of elders and missionaries.

Then there were the elders and deacons; the first tended to look after spiritual matters and the latter, practical matters and all had to be upstanding men of glowing character, the job description provided in detail in Titus 1, 1 Timothy 3 and 1 Timothy 5. Yes, just two Church offices – elders and deacons. So what about the rest – the priests and pastors and bishops etc? For a start, the priestly role is very much Old Testament, so the Catholics and Orthodox Church of today have created an office of the Church that has absolutely no function at all in the New Covenant of Jesus Christ. As for pastors and bishops, despite these roles being cranked up these days to positions of prestige and authority, they are, in fact, just glorified elders! Please explain ...

A modern-day pastor is viewed as the figurehead, the chief focus, for a church, with responsibilities usually wider than just the pastoral aspect. In the days of Peter and Paul the role was more commonly known as *shepherd*, with the job of "protecting the flock". A pastor (shepherd) was not seen as a job title as it is now, simply an elder who specialised in keeping an eye over fellow Christians. Similarly a bishop (also known as overseer), may be a grand title these days, but then was simply an elder who had oversight of the flock. Nowadays, both roles seem to have climbed a rung on a hierarchy of power, with a pastor seen as being in charge of a church and a bishop having authority over a collection of churches. The truth is simpler, with the humbler origins of shepherd and overseer of a single flock.

For the final word on this subject we have an insight into the interchangeableness of these titles and the realisation that the first apostles were more concerned with the *functions of the office* rather than the office itself. Here's what Peter wrote:

To the elders among you, I appeal as a fellow elder, a witness of Christ's sufferings and one who also will share in the glory to be revealed: Be shepherds of God's flock that is under your care, serving as overseers – not because you must, but because you are willing, as God wants you to be; not greedy for money,

but eager to serve; not lording it over those entrusted to you, but being examples to the flock.
(1 Peter 5:1-3)

The other church office was that of deacon. It was in Acts 6:1-7 that we read that the apostles needed others to take on more practical responsibilities, to wait on tables (or specifically, arrange food distribution) while they preached. So they chose seven men, so gifted. These were the first deacons. This doesn't mean that these were to be the stay-at-home unsung toilers, while others did the exciting stuff. Two of these first deacons were Stephen, a man who did great wonders and miraculous signs among the people and Philip, the great evangelist and miracle worker in Samaria. God's gifts to us are not dependent on our position, they are freely given to all.

Now we have looked at Church organisation, what about timetables? When did this early Church meet? A major clue is here:

On the first day of the week we came together to break bread. Paul spoke to the people and, because he intended to leave the next day, kept on talking until midnight.
(Acts 20:7)

The *first day of the week* is a Sunday, by our reckoning, but not by theirs – unless you are prepared to believe that Paul spoke continuously for over 14 hours! They were just being *Biblical*. The Bible tells that a "religious" day starts at sunset, at the first glimmer of the evening.

God called the light "day," and the darkness he called "night." And there was evening and there was morning – the first day.
(Genesis 1:5)

It is a sabbath of rest for you, and you must deny yourselves. From the evening of the ninth day of the month until the following

evening you are to observe your sabbath.
(Leviticus 23:32)

So the early Church may have met on the first day of the week, but it was actually a *Saturday* evening. Why would they have met then? An interesting and believable reason has been put forwards, which takes me quite nicely into the next point I wish to make about the early Church – where else did they meet?

The Jewish Sabbath, then as now, starts at sundown on a Friday until three stars appear in the sky on Saturday night. At the time of the early Church there was one communal activity, where Jews met for worship, teaching, prayer and fellowship during the Sabbath. This was the *synagogue*. The first apostles and disciples were synagogue-goers, *even since they became followers of Jesus Christ.* They were still Jews and still identified with their people and worshipped the same God. And, after all, it was in the synagogue where the word of God was read out from scrolls – the home churches would probably not have any scrolls of their own. Finally, it was in the synagogues where evangelism could happen. Let's see if Scripture bears these things out:

At Iconium Paul and Barnabas went as usual into the Jewish synagogue. There they spoke so effectively that a great number of Jews and Gentiles believed.
(Acts 14:1)

After the reading from the Law and the Prophets, the synagogue rulers sent word to them, saying, "Brothers, if you have a message of encouragement for the people, please speak.
(Acts 13:15)

As Paul and Barnabas were leaving the synagogue the people invited them to speak further about these things on the next Sabbath.
(Acts 13:42)

Yes, it really seems that synagogues were great mission grounds for the early Church, with some surprising results.

Crispus, the synagogue ruler, and his entire household believed in the Lord; and many of the Corinthians who heard him believed and were baptised.
(Acts 18:8)

So, if it was normal for those early Jewish believers to continue visiting synagogues on the Sabbath then perhaps it's not beyond the bounds of possibility that, at the end of the Sabbath, on Saturday evening, they would meet up with their brethren in their house church, where they would share, among other things, what they have learned and experienced that day. Remember, the first day of the week, the Lord's Day, started on Saturday evening. So, with that in mind, read on:

On the first day of the week we came together to break bread. Paul spoke to the people and, because he intended to leave the next day, kept on talking until midnight. There were many lamps in the upstairs room where we were meeting. Seated in a window was a young man named Eutychus, who was sinking into a deep sleep as Paul talked on and on. When he was sound asleep, he fell to the ground from the third story and was picked up dead. Paul went down, threw himself on the young man and put his arms around him. "Don't be alarmed," he said. "He's alive!" Then he went upstairs again and broke bread and ate. After talking until daylight, he left. The people took the young man home alive and were greatly comforted.
(Acts 20:7-12)

Now for Paul to talk continuously until midnight, the chances were that he started talking sometimes in the evening i.e. this was an evening service, not a morning one. So, to meet in the evening on the first day of the week, was to meet on a *Saturday* evening. This could very well have been the norm for the early Church. Incidentally Paul definitely *was* a good talker as, after speaking for, say, 3-4 hours, then raising the young man from the dead, then eating, he returned to his sermon and carried on for a few more hours! He must have been a very *very* engaging speaker!

But now I'm going to be radical and suggest that things weren't *quite* what was indicated. Here are the first three verses of that passage, but with a slightly better translation:

> *On the first day of the week we came together to break bread. Paul dialogued with the people and, because he intended to leave the next day, kept on until midnight. There were many lamps in the upstairs room where we were meeting. Seated in a window was a young man named Eutychus, who was sinking into a deep sleep as Paul continued to dialogue with them.*
> (Acts 20:7-9)

Slightly better translation? What's that all about? Aren't all translations true to the original Greek? Well, sometimes the translators, when given a choice between two or three different possible meanings for a Greek word, would tend to arrive at the position most comfortable for them. It's not that they have mistranslated, it's that they may have *flavoured* the meaning.

Look again at the passage. The Greek word in question is *dialegomai*, that could mean "preach", but more correctly could mean "dialogue" or "discuss". The translators preferred the acceptable Church model of Paul giving a sermon, but a better fit would be him leading a group discussion. Hold onto that thought for now, it will make more sense later on.

This has just been a snapshot of what life was probably like for the 1st Century Church, when the original apostles were still alive, guiding and teaching, training and preaching, through miracles, personal examples, exposition and letters. But Peter, Paul and the others were bound by the three score and ten years allocated to us all and one by one, their numbers dwindled, usually at the hands of those who feared their message. Then they were all gone.

What was to happen to the Church now …?

How the Plot Was Lost

In the last chapter we had a snapshot of the early Church, *The Way* of the apostles. This should have been the first reel of a blockbuster movie, with the unique story of God becoming man and living on earth and rescuing folk through His sacrificial act. This would have been a story of life from the dead for the whole World, a sweeping story of hope and love and salvation, of individuals touched by the message and passing it on, from generation to generation until, in the final reel, all are saved and living in eternity with Father God.

Yes, The Great Director wrote the script, but, by and large, we never followed it. A rogue contributor inserted spoilers into the plot, to confuse, distract and lead the cast into other directions. Millions of minds were enticed away by false religions and philosophies, even more were trapped by their physical appetites. But these weren't the only casualties. Worst of all were the subtle attacks, leaving the victim innocently unaware. These came in the guise of ideas, celebrations of human cleverness, birthed in Ancient Greece. They came well recommended, rubber-stamped by many of the Church Fathers, as complementary, even enhancements, to *The Way* of the apostles. But these ideas were, in reality, spiritual parasites, insinuating themselves into the DNA of pure Christian doctrine, with one single objective ... divide and conquer. Doctrines became debatable, leading to deviations and divisions, heresies and denominations. A veritable riot of mixed metaphor! It gets worse ...

This process has continued unabated for nearly 2,000 years. As a result, it seems our only memory of *The Way* is of an old dog-eared black-and-white Polaroid picture, drifting on the breeze as it spirals downwards into the gutter, to be trodden on and forgotten as an irrelevance. A far off memory of a time that we can never return to ... or can we?

What started up as a single group of twelve apostles and friends has exploded into thousands of fragments, cascading through history to our present age. Is it possible to piece it all together again and return to the very start of it all, or is this a fruitless task, made so by human progress and advancement? Have we migrated to a new land, more suited to our current lives or is there a way to reverse the sweep of time and re-engage in every way with the Church of Peter and Paul?

Things rarely stay the same. History shows us that we are restless creatures, always on the move. Empires come, have a look around, generally create havoc, then dwindle as others have their day. Men of thought and deed create new ways of living and dying. The great forces of "progress" trundle along, thrusting forth new ideas and scattering the old in their wake. Populations move, driven by conquest or material need and God looks on and must wonder, *why couldn't they have just obeyed me and stayed in the garden?*

But we are what we are. We are a product of our history and there's no way we can change the past. We may not be able to change it, but we can certainly *learn* from it. So what did those Greeks actually do to spoil the plot?

In my last book (*How the Church lost The Truth* ...) I covered much of the background of how the *dualism* of Plato and *rationalism* of Aristotle did so much damage to the Church. But how did these ideas translate into the actions of the early Church? We've already looked at the "Acts of the apostles"; what were the *Acts of the Church Fathers*?

First a little glimpse into one facet of human nature. In *the Lord of the Flies*, a plane crashes on a deserted island and the only survivors are a group of children. They quickly organise themselves into groups with leaders, but re-organise themselves differently as some personalities start to dominate and seek power or influence. The film *The Admirable Crichton* is loosely similar, in a gentler way, replacing children with a cross-section of the English class system. The TV series *Lost* is yet another variation on the theme.

The issue is our tendency to organise ourselves into pecking orders or hierarchies, based usually on the forcefulness of the personalities of those higher up the chain. Of course, Christians are not exempt from this kind of behaviour, in fact some seem to absolutely revel in it!

The pattern set by the first apostles had been so simple. They would lend a hand and help get a local church started, including the appointment of a group of mature Christians, called *elders*, who would teach and oversee the flock and some other responsible folk, *deacons*, who would look after practical issues. The elders would specialise according to gift and ability – some would be pastors (shepherds), some bishops (overseers), some teachers, some preachers – all of equal status. Each local church would function in the same way, with the only link between them an informal one, defined by human relationships and mutual support. Then came the Gentile Church fathers, and everything changed …

We need to know how the Church became transformed from a collection of equals, each functioning according to gift and calling to the great hierarchical structures of today. For instance, the modern Catholic Church has a hierarchy to rival a multinational corporation, from Pope, to cardinals, patriarchs, archbishops, bishops, prelates, archdeacons, parish priests, all resplendent in their clerical garb, looking down at the great unwashed, the common laity, you and me (if we were Catholics). The Anglicans are almost as bad, in fact just about every denomination has some sort of ladder of self-importance in place.

As soon as the restraining influence of the first apostles was gone with the death of the last one, John, this tendency began to creep into the Church. Ignatius was John's disciple in Antioch and, on the way to martyrdom in Rome, wrote the following in a letter to the church in Ephesus:

"Now the more any one sees the bishop keeping silence, the more ought he to revere him. For we ought to receive every one whom the Master of the house sends to be over His household, as we would do Him that sent him. It is manifest, therefore, that we should look upon the bishop even as we would upon the Lord Himself".
(Epistle to the Ephesians 6:1)

Pardon me? We should look upon the bishop even as we would upon the Lord Himself! The bishop in place of Jesus himself? How had the role of bishop, an elder with responsibilities of overseeing the flock of a single church, been so elevated in so short a time? The first hierarchy had appeared, with the bishop lording it over the presbyter (another elder, usually translated as priest), the deacon and the layman. He makes this clear here:

"As therefore the Lord does nothing without the Father, for says He, "I can of mine own self do nothing", so do ye, neither presbyter, nor deacon, nor layman, do anything without the bishop. Nor let anything appear commendable to you which is destitute of his approval".
(Epistle to the Magnesians 7)

So why had a hierarchy appeared, so soon after the time of the first apostles and so contrary to the picture painted by Scripture?

It wasn't just all about Ignatius, though, as we also have writings from another early Church Father, Clement of Rome. In his letter to the church in Corinth, he makes a very telling statement:

For thus saith the Scripture in a certain place, "I will appoint their bishops in righteousness, and their deacons in faith."
(Chapter 42)

He was quoting here from Isaiah 60:17, but he quoted wrong!

Instead of bronze I will bring you gold, and silver in place of iron. Instead of wood I will bring you bronze, and iron in place of stones. I will make peace your governor and righteousness your ruler.
(Isaiah 60:17)

This was mischievous, to say the least, and helps to illustrate that, outside of Holy Scripture, much of what we read is going to be coloured by human ambition or agenda. Clement has equated bishops and deacons with the "ruling classes" and helped to set the theme for generations to come. He was also the first to refer to "ordinary" Christians as *laity* (in Chapter 40*)*, exposing a divide, borne out of the duality taught by Plato (as explained in "How the Church lost the Way ..."), that was henceforth going to be a feature of Church history. The *clergy* – deacons, priests, bishops etc. – were to be the special "spiritual" Christians, as if the following Scripture referred to them only:

But you are a chosen people, a royal priesthood, a holy nation, a people belonging to God, that you may declare the praises of him who called you out of darkness into his wonderful light.
(1 Peter 2:9)

Again I ask the question, why did this structure and hierarchy appear in the early Church? The most likely reason was in the fight against heresy, deviant beliefs that had polluted the Church mainly through the attempt to reconcile Biblical faith with pagan Greek philosophy. By elevating the bishop to a position of "God-like" authority, it was hoped that this would quell these regional outbreaks of division in the Church. Perhaps it did, but the cure soon became the problem.

It now became the bishop's job to administer the Lord's Supper, to preach, to conduct baptisms and marriage ceremonies, to lead prayers, look after discipline and generally dish out advice. So a 2nd century bishop was much like a 21st century vicar, but the Bible speaks of neither.

Now you are the body of Christ, and each one of you is a part of it. And in the church God has appointed first of all apostles, second prophets, third teachers, then workers of miracles, also those having gifts of healing, those able to help others, those with gifts of administration, and those speaking in different kinds of tongues.
(1 Corinthians 12:27-28)

Then there was a shift. Bishops were elevated in rank, given responsibilities for groups of churches, even whole cities (or the whole World, in the case of the Pope – the *Bishop* of Rome) and their place was taken by *priests*.

So, priests, eh? Isn't the priesthood something out of the Old Testament, done away with by the death of Jesus? No, there is still a High Priest …

Therefore, since we have a great high priest who has gone through the heavens, Jesus the Son of God, let us hold firmly to the faith we profess.
(Hebrews 4:14)

And there are ordinary priests, too …

… you also, like living stones, are being built into a spiritual house to be a holy priesthood offering spiritual sacrifices acceptable to God through Jesus Christ.
(1 Peter 2:5)

... and has made us to be a kingdom and priests to serve his God and Father – to him be glory and power for ever and ever! Amen.
(Revelation 1:6)

Yes, Jesus Christ is the great High Priest, having made the ultimate and lasting sacrifice for our sins, he is able to intercede for us with God the Father.

Now there have been many of those priests, since death prevented them from continuing in office; but because Jesus lives forever, he has a permanent priesthood. Therefore he is able to save completely those who come to God through him, because he always lives to intercede for them.
(Hebrews 7:23-25)

And all who profess faith in him are his priests, each of us gaining access to the High Priest, offering our sacrifices of praise (Hebrews 13:15) and our bodies as living sacrifices to him (Romans 12:1).

So where do these *other* priests come from? We get some clues from the writings of Cyprian of Carthage, in the 3rd Century:

"For neither have heresies arisen, nor have schisms originated, from any other source than from this, that God's priest is not obeyed; nor do they consider that there is one person for the time priest in the Church, and for the time judge in the stead of Christ; whom, if, according to divine teaching, the whole fraternity should obey, no one would stir up anything against the college of priests; no one, after the divine judgment, after the suffrage of the people, after the consent of the co-bishops, would make himself a judge, not now of the bishop, but of God. No one would rend the Church by a division of the unity of Christ."
(Epistle 54)

So bishops by then had been promoted to leadership of a network of churches and a whole caste of middle-men, priests, had sprung up. The ordinary Christians were now told that they – mere laity – were not meant to approach God directly, instead all of the "spiritual" duties – confession of sin, communion, prayer etc – were now performed on their behalf, by the clergy, specifically the *priest*.

The rest of Church history, right up to modern times, is just a variation and development of this basic theme. Whether it is the vast hierarchies of the Catholic, Anglican and Orthodox Church, or the structures of the various modern movements – apostolic, house church etc. – the middle men, or intermediaries, are still with us, replacing the simple truth for every Christian. As a reminder:

> ... *you also, like living stones, are being built into a spiritual house to be a holy priesthood offering spiritual sacrifices acceptable to God through Jesus Christ.*
> (1 Peter 2:5)

Talking about spiritual houses, our next task is to investigate how "church" began life as a collection of called-out people meeting in homes, but ended up as a vastly adorned building containing all sorts of people. Was it expansion in numbers that forced them out of their homes into larger halls? Was it the lack of space in homes for special seating for the clergy? Was it because they suddenly had a lot of cash and decided to invest in real estate?

To borrow an image from the evolutionists, when did the first Christians emerge blinking from the safety of their homes and book some property viewings with the ecclesiastical estate agent?

When was the first church built? Interestingly not until the 4th Century. This means that, even though by then we had the beginning of the hierarchies and the rise of the clergy, they were still crammed into living rooms in folk's homes for at least a couple of hundred years. So the first few Popes in Rome were in much humbler surroundings than their counterparts in later times (though the title itself was not used until the 3rd Century). No doubt this was far better for their soul, if not for their self-image. You can imagine such a conversation held at that time: "Come on Cornelius, others may think you're a big shot but in this house you'll be on the washing-up rota like everyone else!"

That's not the mental image we have of the churches in those first couple of centuries – the great congregations in Antioch, Ephesus, Rome and Alexandria. They were all house churches, which is not surprising when we realise that much of that period was a time of intense Roman persecution. So it makes sense that the first purpose-built churches are not going to appear in the Roman world until things had become a lot safer.

Then, near the start of the 4th Century, came Emperor Constantine, the fiend who posed as a friend of Christianity. As described in my last two books, he not only secularised the Christian faith, but formalised the persecution of the Jews as a matter of Church policy. He made Christianity the State religion and, by doing so, created an environment for power-mongers, chancers and out-and-out villains to flourish, under the guise of religious practitioners. The clergy, so persecuted by the previous Emperor Diocletian, eventually became the persecutors, although this was disguised as protecting the doctrine at the time. One of Constantine's weapons was the new programme of church building that he initiated.

In the city that bears his name, Constantinople, he commissioned the building of "holy" meeting places, both pagan and Christian, no doubt to cover all bases. This building programme was repeated in Rome, Jerusalem and all over the Empire, the major churches mainly being built over the tombs of dead saints, because of the supposed power of these "sacred places", an idea that was thoroughly pagan.

Now Christians were enticed out of their home churches and told that, as the Emperor had converted, one now had to look to him and his clergy rather than the Holy Spirit on such matters as where to meet. This was the birth of State Christianity, still with us today, albeit in the watered-down form of the Church of England and now *being Church* had subtly changed to *going to church*. These Christian meeting places were based on Greek civic buildings, the *basilica*, a perfect design to accommodate active performers and passive onlookers. Any sense of interactivity or personal involvement was going to be squeezed out of one's "church experience". The stage was literally set for the clergy to "do their thing".

Suddenly, people who had been pagans for their whole lives were told to throw away their idols because they were Christians now and had to join real Christians and congregate every week in these new churches. They witnessed, from their seats near the back, the awesome mystery of Holy Communion, an activity of such great awe and power that it could only be administered in a dry and solemn ritual, performed by a special person in strange clothing, at a sacred place in the centre of the room called an altar. This person, called a bishop, sat on an elevated throne, surrounded by lower ranked members of the clergy and, at one point in the proceedings, was to give a long speech, called a sermon. The warm, supportive and godly gatherings of the early Church had become a ritualised costume drama acted out by career churchmen. The job of the congregation was simply to listen and only speak when told to.

This was the normal Christian experience in the 4th Century, once the Church had ceased to be a collective of called-out believers in the risen Christ and was now the place where citizens – believers and unbelievers – met together under State-authorised worship. And, you can say, this is the experience in many churches to this day.

Now, in the last chapter, we noticed that the actual Greek word, *kyriakon*, that transliterates as "church", only appears twice in the New Testament, with the meaning, "belonging to the Lord". Yet the word that is commonly translated as "church" is e*kklesia*, meaning "called out". Why aren't we called out into "ekkleses", then? This was a question posed by William Tyndale, in the 16th Century. He was a Protestant who was the first to translate much of the Greek and Hebrew Scriptures of the Bible into English and ended his life burnt at the stake as a heretic by the Catholics. (By that time the definition of heresy had changed somewhat from the early days of the Church, into something political and sinister.)

Tyndale saw what had happened to Christendom, now a ritualised, materialistic corporation administered from Rome and propagated through a network of richly adorned churches and cathedrals by purveyors of greed and faulty theology. So when he turned to the word *ekklesia*, with the original meaning of the *people* of God, rather than translate it as "church", as everyone else did, he chose the word "congregation", focussing on the people, the *called-out ones*. This attack on the Church authorities brought him into conflict with them and no doubt contributed to his demise. Nevertheless, the *King James Bible* drew on his work, but *ekklesia* was translated as "church". Most subsequent translations have done so too. So, ever since, Western Christianity has been viewed as more about what goes on *inside* these buildings, hidden and insulated from the real world, rather than the activities of Christians outside the building.

So we have seen how "church" may have started as *called-out ones*, but, once Greek thinking and personal ambition had been added to the mix, it had reverse metamorphosised, from the beautiful free butterfly of the earliest expressions to the ugly caterpillar of State control.

A question demands to be asked. *Is this process reversible? Can we return to those exciting days of Peter and Paul and the first apostles, or have we just moved too far away ... ?*

No Going Back?

So, is there a way back? Surely too much has happened in the intervening 2000 years to make this possible? Society has moved on – what can a sophisticated technologically-advanced post-modern civilisation have in common with a far-flung primitive outpost of the corrupt Roman empire, when woman were viewed as mere chattels and brutality ruled? Yes, our bodies inhabit different times, totally different environments, but what of our inner life? What is the state of our souls? How has human progress and technological advancement affected the "inner man"?

Have we learned to get on with each other? No, witness the First and Second World Wars and the escalating violence that stalks our modern World.

Have we overcome the brutal ways we treat each other? No, witness Auschwitz, Hiroshima, 9/11.

Have we solved the problems of the human condition? No, witness the rise in racism, unwanted pregnancies, hate crimes, poverty (despite a worldwide surplus of food), environmental damage etc. etc.

So, what's changed? Actually, in things that matter ... nothing! 21st Century man (and woman) has as much need of the transforming Gospel of Jesus Christ as those who lived with him in the 1st Century.

But, still, we can't totally ignore two thousand years of Church history. I suggest that there is an *elephant in the room* for any modern fellowship trying to recreate the original Church in their living room, an unavoidable issue that needs to be addressed at some point.

Two thousand years of Greek thinking

It's in our DNA. Two thousand years of being taught to think in a certain way is very significant. The Greek mindset (more of this in the next section of this book) may have given us scientific progress and a soft easy life (when's the last time you had to hunt for your food, or rely on a harvest or fetch water from a well?) but it does not provide a natural interface for our dealings with God. It is not comfortable with the supernatural, with the World beyond our senses, with the spiritual World where we meet with God. And, especially, it does not provide us with the correct tools for understanding God's Word, The Bible. We need to begin to think and act *Biblically*. Easier said than done. More of this in the next two sections of this book.

Now we hear again and again of churches and fellowships that declare, *we need to get back to the original Church!* This was the rallying cry of the original *house church movement* in the 1970s. They called themselves *charismatic restorationists* and intended to create churches closer to the New Testament forms of government and organisation. Very soon came splits over such issues as how to engage with the culture, attitudes to women and theological interpretations and hierarchies were created, in the form of networks of churches and leadership structures. Nowadays, these churches have became mini-denominations of their own, though not all of them. I am aware of at least one group of house churches that have functioned in their own quiet way much the same for the last thirty years, without succumbing to the need to create networks and hierarchies.

Other groups have also reacted against the state of the modern Church and have gone "back to basics", but, bearing in mind that there may be successes we don't hear of for very good reasons (they have no desire for fame or publicity), few seem to have succeeded. Why is this? I have already suggested a possible reason; the curse of Greek thinking. But some commentators have suggested other possibilities.

They say that the reason why we can't return to the heady days of old is that the church of Peter and Paul in the Book of Acts was unique, a one-off, extraordinary period of time, ring-fenced by God to get the ball rolling. The reasoning is that He had to pull out all of the stops to ensure that such a momentum of power and deed would be built up in such a short period of time, to drive the Christian Movement well into the future. For these commentators, the unavoidable evidence for the uniqueness of that first period of Church history, is that it has *never been repeated*. Of course that doesn't mean that it *could* never be repeated, just that, in their view, it hasn't happened yet. They would also say that the Book of Acts just features the highlights over a longish period of time, that miracles and marvellous events didn't exactly happen every day and that much of the time could have been quite boring and unexceptional. *Hey, how do they know, were they there?* A weak argument, I think.

But the greatest focus is on the apostles themselves. They look at the title – The Acts of the Apostles – and say, *hey, it was the apostles who did all the exciting stuff and surely they are not around any more?* Interestingly, early manuscripts suggest that the actual title was *Acts of Apostles*, suggesting that the "acts" recorded were not the *only* acts and that it wasn't just *the* apostles that were doing them. Were the apostles at that time unique in world history, endowed with powers and insights that never have and never will be repeated?

There are some who believe that is so and they would take it further. They suggest that the Church of the first apostles was so special that God ensured it could never happen again by *pulling the plug* on the spiritual gifts once the last apostle had died. And what a can of worms is thus opened. To say this is a contentious issue is a whopping understatement. This is a battleground far deadlier and extensive than any that I discussed in my last book, *How the Church lost The Truth.* It has big hitters on both sides, with an arsenal of long words and torturous definitions. It is cessationism vs continuationism, with the former boasting as many flavours as an ice lolly; classical, full, strong, moderate, principled or empirical; *you pays your money, you takes your choice.*

Do we want to go there and analyse each nuance? No, we don't. First we look at what would motivate those folk who believe that God would take away His gifts from His Church, once the anchor was securely in place. Imagine you were living in Europe in the 16th Century and were writing an essay on *The Catholic Church and the Spiritual Gifts.* Here are some observations you would have made:

There were mortal men on Earth, called Popes, apparently uniquely authorised as God's representatives, to interpret His word and to formulate Church policy. The Church also claimed the authority to buy and sell *indulgences*, providing an easier path in the hereafter in return for hard earned cash. Miracles were apparently rife in Catholic history, specifically in the lives of "saints", especially holy people who operated within the realm of supernatural signs and wonders. Saint Joseph of Cupertino used to fly around while praying (patron saint of pilots). St Anthony used to preach to fish and mules (who responded). St Nicholas of Tolentino used to bless pieces of bread, which would then heal people. And the list goes on and on.

While you were making your observations, others were reacting in more direct ways. They were *protesting*, the Reformation had arrived. Many of them reacted fiercely against these Catholic excesses and strange claims and a great thrust of this attack was on theological grounds. If they could prove *Biblically* that all spiritual gifts had ceased since the age of the first apostles, then the whole foundation of Catholic belief – with its strange doctrines and even stranger miraculous claims – would be exposed as false. Thus was born *cessationism.*

Yet this was a reaction to the very real corruptions in the mainstream (Catholic) Church of the day. It was always going to be a case of, *this can't be right so let's go back to the Bible and try to prove this.* This approach was always going to attract accusations of *eisegesis,* the act of reading your own thoughts and ideas into Scripture, even if you have a just cause and are just seeking to defend the very Bible itself.

We, too, can fall into the same trap. We can also see the excesses that, ironically, have been birthed from within the protestant denominations, namely the growth of self-proclaimed "apostles" and "prophets", particularly from what has been termed the *New Apostolic Reformation* (NAR), in the USA. Here are a group of folk who, despite declaring themselves a *Reformed* movement, are closer than they realise to the medieval Catholic Church, in terms of hierarchies of authority and "new revelations", ranging from promised revivals (that have been *just round the corner* since the 1980s!) and miraculous claims every bit as wacky as Catholic saints of old.

This may tempt us to make the same sweeping proclamations as the early Reformers. *There are currently many "apostles" taking authority, making proclamations and building hierarchies and personal empires, so if we can prove that the office of apostle was done away with in the 1st Century ... that will show them!*

So, who's right, who's wrong? Can the whole Catholic chain of command and spiritual claims be demolished Biblically? Can we confound the modern "apostolic movement" by disproving their existence Biblically? Or is this just another pointless exercise, just another endless debate between Christians who brandish their Bibles and confidently state, "The Bible says ..."

Leaving the theological arguments to others (and I'll explain why, later on), it's always fruitful to consider consequences of views and opinions, rather than the views and opinions themselves.

Let's consider the scenario that God took away all spiritual gifts in the 1st Century. No more miracles, healing, prophecy, speaking in tongues and no more apostles or prophets to exercise these gifts. The only way God speaks to us now is through His Word, The Bible. It is totally sufficient in every way to help us to deal with whatever may come our way in life. Anything *extra* to this, in terms of dreams, visions, prophecies, leadings from God, words of knowledge are invalid and to be ignored.

If this were the case then there has not been a single God-authorised healing since the 1st Century. Neither has God interfered directly in our world, in terms of guidance or judgement, whether through His manipulation of natural events or through that *still, small voice* to individuals. Every revival is to be denied, including the Welsh Revival of 1904, when men fainted with the enormity of their sins, flattened by the Holy Spirit, simply just by walking past a church. Every Church leader who spoke in tongues or witnessed healings and miracles, including Martyn Lloyd Jones, Rees Howells or Derek Prince is to be categorised at best as deluded and at worst as deluding.

To me it smacks a little of Deism, the idea that God got everything going, wrote down the rules and regulations in the Bible then thrust it in our hands saying, *there it is, all you need, you're on your own now, I'm off ...*, before sailing away into the sunset.

On the other hand, if the spiritual gifts continue, we must wonder why there are so few documented examples of their use (outside of some ridiculous claims in the "lives of the saints") in the early Church, the times of the Church Fathers. And, by way of contrast, why they seem to currently run unchecked, with 1 in 3 American Christians, in a current survey, declaring that they have heard directly from God. Here is a selection of shenanigans promoted by a popular "prophetic" mailing list:

(This person) ... has a supernatural gift to help you tap into God's miraculous power. Tune in as she gives insight on how to release the anointing within you, pray the kind of prayers that produce miracles, and begin experiencing the supernatural for yourself!

(This person) ... sees into the future with such amazing accuracy! Find out what's in store for America, President Barack Obama, and the Middle East.

There are angels standing to attention with your personal addresses written on them that will be released to set up camp round about your dwelling place, to deliver family members far and near.

At the beginning of the year, the Spirit of the Lord spoke profoundly to me that this was the year where God would strategically shift members of the Body of Christ, moving them into their places of inheritance and prosperity, divinely orchestrating circumstances so that the wealth that we are destined to possess would be transferred into our lives.

Come and experience these new realms of Glory as we step through the open door and into the third heaven where we go from Glory to Glory to Glory. It's in this glory realm that all your needs will be met and miracles take place.

Surely it's enough to make cessationists of us all!

So, where does this leave us? Dare we suggest that, these days, anything goes or do we equally dare that, these days, nothing goes? If the cessationists are correct then there is no way we can go *back to the roots* and create a modern church that emulates the church of Peter and Paul, because we are no longer running at full voltage, barely enough power to pop out some prayers, let alone charge up a room of glossalalists (look that one up yourselves)!

I have tried to remain impartial so far, but now have to take a position. As much as many in the charismatic movement have taken great liberties in the freedoms of our faith, I don't believe God has hamstrung us by withdrawing His spiritual gifts. I don't believe He gave us the great narratives in the New Testament, of wonderful miraculous deeds and demonstrations of His power, just to tease us. He's not saying, *you can look, but you can't touch.* It may well have been that every spiritual gift available was needed to establish the first Church, but arguably, the modern Church is assaulted by unprecedented pressures – from society, from other religions and lifestyle and, most sadly, *from within the fold* (hence the need for this book ☺). Would God have left us powerless, even though some have opted to misuse that power?

No, I believe we can return in every way to the form of the very first Church. In fact, some have tried and perhaps would have succeeded … if it weren't for other Christians.

And this is where we go next …

The Way, Revisited

I have been greatly troubled as I delved deeper and deeper into Church history. In my earlier books, focussing on interactions between Christians and Jews, all I saw was the nastiness, of the expulsions and persecutions. In my latter books, focussing on the damage done by Greek thinking, again it was the bad stuff that came to the forefront, the corruptions and the disunity and the wars over doctrine. I couldn't help but think, *where was the true Christian witness during this troubled history? Where was the authentic Gospel message during the Dark Ages, or at other times when Christendom was stifling the life out of the faith? Where were the faithful remnant to keep the torch flickering?*

The story so far was that, once upon a time, there was God's authentic Church, founded by the apostles who had learned at the feet of Jesus himself. Then the apostles died and new ideas from Greece were allowed to mix with the pure doctrine of the Christian faith. Out of this tainted root came the established Western Church, the State Church of Augustine and Aquinas and the Catholics. When the Protestants appeared on the scene it was not from without, but from within; it was a *reformation* of the existing structures, not a spanking new broom sweeping clean. Yet out of all of this, the Gospel message has still reached us, despite the bumps and bangs of nearly 2,000 years of doctrinal turbulence.

My question is this, *why didn't the pagan seed from Greek thinking completely blot out the true message of the Gospel?* We saw the consequences of faulty theology, through the crusades, the inquisition, the religious wars and the hatred and conflicts that characterised so much of Church history. Even the Protestants eventually succumbed to the subtle perversions of Greek philosophy, so how was the true Gospel preserved?

Then I dug deeper. It led me into some serious study and Holy Spirit nudges and a realisation that, since the days of the Church Fathers, there have in fact been two Church movements. I am not talking of Catholic vs. Protestant, or Roman Catholic vs. Greek Orthodox. It is far more clear cut, it is the Church tainted by Greek philosophy vs. the Church un-tainted by Greek philosophy. The first Church is basically the one with roots in the ancient Roman Empire and includes the Catholics and the vast majority of Protestant denominations. Although it is a Church compromised to a certain extent by Greek philosophy, it is not a Church that has been completely powerless as, through God's grace, many have found true salvation within these religious structures.

But it's the second Church, the one untainted by Greek philosophy, that interests me. If we can identify it, it would provide a direct link to the original Church of the first apostles, the Church of The Way. So, here the story begins ... with an apology!

But what a fascinating story emerges. They say that history tends to be written by the victors; you very rarely get the *other point of view*, that of the marginalised, the dissenting voices, the vanquished. In my previous book, *How the Church lost The Truth*, I referred to the 2nd Century Christian, *Montanus* rather negatively as a "heretic who heard voices". It appears that both he and his most exalted follower, *Tertullian*, attracted a bad press from the main-stream Christian historians, because they spoke against many of the excesses of the Church of their day, hence the claims of heresy. Also, "hearing voices", seems to be a reaction against Montanus' prophetic gift and his teaching on the Second Coming of Christ was most unpopular, as was his view that Easter should be dated according to the Jewish calendar. So perhaps he wasn't quite as bad as I painted him. In my defence, I concluded that Tertullian was one of the good guys, as one who resisted the mixing of Greek philosophy with the Christian faith. "What has Athens to do with Jerusalem?" he once said.

A few words about Tertullian. He was a strong moralist, for him actions were as important as words. He also wrote a lot of words, a fiery writer well versed in the noble art of sarcasm and puns. He wrote on doctrine, but also on everyday stuff, like marriage, clothing and cosmetics, a sort of *Martha Stewart meets Martin Luther*. But when he became a *Montanist* he withdrew from the world and refused to compromise with its ways, preferring to make a stand against the culture of the day.

He takes our story forwards (though, actually *backwards*) through this quote:

"Regions in Britain that have never been penetrated by Roman arms have received the religion of Christ."

Tertullian tells us that Christianity had reached the British Isles before the Romans got there. The implication here is that Britain could have received the true faith, unadulterated by the Greek thinking that had polluted the Christian faith in Europe and the Middle East. So, where was this found and how did it get there?

It appears that the gospel had reached our islands before the Romans turned up, but it's unclear how. In fact, up to a dozen different suggestions have been made, from personal visits by Jesus, Andrew, Joseph of Arimathea or Paul, to missionary endeavours by, among others, the Galatians and the Coptic Church in Egypt, to the more mundane (and probably correct) activities of merchants and soldiers. The fact is that, by the time Augustine (another one!) arrived on these shores in the 6th Century AD and was proclaimed the first Archbishop of Canterbury, there was already an indigenous form of the faith known as *Celtic Christianity*.

When I learnt this my heart sank a little. Wasn't Celtic Christianity a bit flaky, a touch of the New Age, heavy on mysticism and sacred spaces? It seems that modern interpretations owe as much to the traditions and views of the intervening years as they do to the actual events in the early Church years. Further investigation revealed that early Celtic Christianity was marked by its fierce independence, its missionary zeal, its centres of education, its reliance on the Bible rather than traditions of men and its own way of calculating the date of Easter! All of these are significant pointers to a faith a lot purer and *Biblical* than that constructed by the Greek Church Fathers.

There's a tiny island called Iona, off the coast of Scotland, a popular tourist destination, particularly for those of a religious bent. The trouble is that your religion is going to have to be rather bent in order to appreciate the spirituality currently on offer there. It features what is known as the Iona Community, diplomatically known as an ecumenical establishment, where you can explore alternative creation … and recreation, Celtic and male spirituality and Palestinian liberation issues. All good examples of *reconstructed* Celtic Christianity.

Which is all a bit of a shame, as Iona was one of the first places in the whole of these British Isles to really experience authentic Biblical Christianity, which spread throughout Scotland. One man brought this Gospel, this Good News untainted by the *Greek* additions, to Iona. He was an Irishman called Columba, who arrived in AD 563, after a dispute over a manuscript, which led to a kerfuffle. It was said that his arrival on the island was a personal act of penance for the blood that was shed in the dispute.

Columba established a Christian community on Iona that was very different from what was becoming the norm in Europe in the 6th Century AD, as it entered the *Dark Ages*. He had already planted forty one similar communities in Ireland, but none of them would have such far-reaching influence as this one on Iona.

Here was real community, under the benevolent direction of the Abbot, of whom Columba was the first. Members of this community were allowed to marry, unlike their counterparts on mainland Europe, who were constricted by the Platonism that had infected their faith. They were extremely Bible literate and were taught to memorise whole passages of Scripture. They also only baptised those who professed faith and celebrated the death and resurrection of Jesus according to the Hebrew calendar.

From this base a relentless period of evangelism was launched, leading to the creating of around sixty similar communities in Scotland before Columba's death. Much has been written about Columba, most of it by his biographer, the ninth Abbot of Iona, who wrote many years later. Such was the obvious hero-worship, that it may be difficult to separate truth from legend, so you have to take some of the following with a pinch of salt, mindful that Columba must have been extremely remarkable just on the basis of his achievements.

He was profoundly persuasive and a charismatic leader, who slept with a rock for a pillow, had a healing and deliverance ministry, was as bold as Elijah in his confrontations with the Druids and was at one with nature, even rebuking the Loch Ness monster on one occasion (the monster hasn't been the same since!)

But the arrival of Augustine to these shores, within a year of Columba's death, was to signal the beginning of the end of this independent expression of the Christian faith and Britain was eventually sucked into the paganised Roman Catholic system.

So what happened to the pure faith of the apostles in the meantime? There surely had to be a surviving remnant somewhere?

This is where it gets interesting or frustrating, depending on your perspective. As I've said earlier, history tends to be written by the victors, by the powers-that-be, by the established authorities. In the case of the battles in the Church, any group that defied the various State Churches tended to be denounced as heretics and their written material burned. So it is difficult to find an impartial historical witness for any expression of Christianity other than the Greek-tainted party-line of official Christendom. A good place to start is to investigate the groups that were hunted, denounced, persecuted and tortured at the hands of the Inquisition or the early Crusades. If they came to the attention of the Popes, the chances were that they were promoting a "different Gospel" to the corrupted version that had been synthesised by the philosophers and theologians and fed to the masses. This made them worthy of investigation.

One such group was the *Waldenses*. Because of the venomous persecution it suffered at the hands of the established Church, there is a vagueness about its history, due to most of its writings being destroyed. There is even some revisionism, promoted by the Catholic Church, claiming that the group only appeared in the later Middle Ages, named after a certain Peter Waldo (as claims the Wikipedia entry), but the truth seems to be that its origins go much further back than that, probably right back to the apostolic times of the 1st Century, providing us with an unbroken link with the authentic Church of the first apostles.

If this is true, then this is exciting indeed, but there was a price to pay, as we shall soon see. This group lived in the valleys of the alpine regions of Northern Italy. They may have shared a country with the Roman Catholics, but they couldn't have been more different. Unsullied by the Greek pagan virus, they had a high view of Holy Scripture, it was their rule of life, it was a living book for them. They firmly believed in preaching and were very good at it, even counting many Catholics among their converts. They also firmly believed that the Pope was not God's representative on Earth and offered allegiance to Jesus Christ alone.

Isn't it sad and telling that the Catholic Encyclopaedia chooses to describe the Waldenses as *an heretical sect that appeared in the second half of the twelfth century* – wrong on both counts! I chuckled at the observation, in the same article, that *among the doctrinal errors which they propagated was the denial of purgatory and of indulgences and prayers for the dead.* There's not much you can say about that!

But it gets worse because the Pope and his advisors decided that the World wasn't big enough for both of them, so one had to go. The Pope was Innocent III, the year was 1215 AD and the event was the Fourth Council of the Lateran. One of the outcomes of this official Catholic Church meeting was that the Waldenses were officially classed as *heretics* and suitable fodder for the *inquisition*.

The next few centuries are a sorry story that parallels the fate of the Jews at the hands of the Catholic Church. It was a period of great persecutions, such as in Merindol, in France, where many hundreds were massacred in 1545.

Another unbroken link from the 1st Century were the *Paulicians,* who took their name from the Apostle Paul and first appeared in Antioch, where Barnabas and Paul preached and where believers were first called *Christians* and where many Jewish Christians migrated after being forced out of Jerusalem. These first Christians were able to migrate northwards to Armenia before the Greek pagan influences took hold. They were resolute in holding firm to the true faith and spoke up against what they saw as unbiblical practices, such as the veneration of relics, the worship of Mary and the saints and the excesses surrounding the Catholic Mass.

Naturally, the Catholics were not amused and the Catholic Encyclopaedia calls them *a dualistic heretical sect, derived originally from Manichaeism.* This is worrying because the Catholics are accusing the Paulicians of a very specific Gnostic heresy that has roots in the dualism of Plato, which, if it is true, would disqualify them as torch-bearers of the true unsullied faith. What we seem to have here is a touch of naughtiness on behalf of the Catholics of that time. In the words of historian, E. H. Broadbent:

"... the churches of believers who called themselves Christians, thus distinguishing themselves from others whom they called "Romans" (Catholics), had always been accused of being Manichaeans, although they declared they were not and complained of the injustice of attributing to them doctrines they did not hold. The frequency with which anything is repeated is no proof that it is true, and since such writings as remain of these Christians contain no trace of Manichaeism, it is only reasonable to believe that they did not hold it."

(The Pilgrim Church, E. H. Broadbent, Gospel Folio Press, 2009 p. 65)

Just playground insults really, delivered by grown-ups, but with deadly consequences because these Paulicians, who held to the true Biblical faith of the early apostles, were, like the Waldenses, mercilessly persecuted by the Catholic Church.

There were many other non-Catholic groups around at the time but it would be wrong to include them all on our list of "good guys", simply because they spoke up against the mainstream Church. Many of them actually were heretical, peddling a corruption of the Christian faith, though a *different* corruption from that practiced by the Catholics of the day. The Catholic Church persecuted them, usually to extinction.

One such group were the *Albigenses* of Southern France. The Catholic Encyclopaedia got it right in their definition this time, calling them *a neo-Manichaean sect*. Although they were marked by their humility and clean living and their disdain for the pomp and corruption of the Catholic Church, their theology was markedly Manichaean. The dualism of Plato had taken hold and they held a distinction between the evil physical world and the pure spiritual world, leading to a totally corrupted view of Christian doctrine and practice. The other group that had appeared in France at around the same time were the *Cathars*, a slang term meant as an insult. They had very similar beliefs to the Albigenses and were eventually wiped out by the Catholic inquisition.

But now back to England. It is the 14th Century and a remarkable man steps onto the stage. This is John Wycliffe, the man who had both the cheek and the grace to translate the Bible from the Latin into English, something unheard of in the Catholic World, where the clear words of Scripture were hidden from the common man. As a result of this, he made a remarkable discovery that was to revolutionise the Christian faith and start a process that led to the sweeping changes of the Reformation many years later. His discovery was … *the Word of God*. Through translating the Bible into English, its very words began to grip his soul and others who followed him. These were the *Lollards*, a derisive name (the 'babblers') given to them by others, a movement labelled a heresy by the Pope and also resisted in this country by the Archbishop of Canterbury. It resulted in the first execution of a layman in England as a heretic; that was John Badby in the 15th Century.

A man called Jerome had listened intently to Wycliffe's sermons in Oxford and took the message of reform for the Catholic Church back to his home city of Prague, in Central Europe. He in turn was listened to by John Huss, a man already influenced by the Waldenses and a new movement was born, the *Hussites*. Huss was immediately excommunicated by the Pope, who also publicly burned Wycliffe's writings, then a few years later, both Jerome and Huss were burned at the stake. This was serious business, indeed.

Many years earlier our old acquaintance Tertullian had said, *the blood of the martyrs is the seed of the Church*. God had ensured that Jerome and Huss didn't die in vain. Around fifty years after John Huss's death a group of his followers, the Bohemian Brethren, morphed into the *Moravians*, one of the first true Protestant Churches. In the early 18th Century, under the leadership of the German nobleman, Count Zinzendorf, they had an encounter with God. On August 13th 1727 the Holy Spirit came down on a group of them with such power that, according to one of them, *"we hardly knew whether we belonged to earth or had already gone to Heaven."* It was a revival.

Out of this came the following: A 24/7 prayer initiative that lasted 100 years, the first ever publication of a daily devotional, the planting of 30 churches, the formation of hundreds of "house churches" and the first ever Protestant mission movement, sending out hundreds of missionaries all over the world. Beat that Toronto, Pensacola, Lakeland!

In 1738, one such missionary, Peter Boehler, had a meeting in London with one John Wesley, informing him that what he needed was true saving faith. Three months later, during a meeting in Aldersgate Street, Wesley relates, *"I felt my heart strangely warmed. I felt I did trust in Christ, Christ alone for salvation, and an assurance was given me that he had taken away my sins, even mine, and saved me from the law of sin and death."*

Thus was born *Methodism*, that started out as a major revival of the Church of England, before becoming a denomination of its own. It is perhaps safe to say that this was the first time the visible and the invisible Churches crossed paths, without bloodshed. The Church of England, a dissident branch of the established Western Church with its roots in Rome and the ideas of the Greek philosophers had collided with the fruit of the long history of the dissident Church, from the Paulicians and Waldenses through to the Lollards, Hussites and Moravians. And the result was ... revival! England and the USA were transformed by the Methodists, who took God to the people, with their relentless open-air preaching. They transformed society from the bottom up.

The Methodists were very disciplined in their religious life and practices, with an emphasis on personal holiness, living the life that they preached (which has not always been the case with Christians). They had regular private devotions and met daily for prayer and Bible study. Eventually they organised themselves into regional groups, stressing discipleship, fellowship and pastoral care. Eventually they split from the Anglicans and became a worldwide movement, still active today, albeit without the doctrinal purity of those early days.

I think my point has been made. Church history is not just about the main stories, the familiar stories promoted by the Catholics and the Protestants and the conflicts between them. Such has been the visible Church, the one with the ear of the historians. But, as I have shown, there has been a second, "alternative" Church in Europe, living in the margins, often hidden out of fear of persecution, but a Church without which the Reformation may never have happened. This is the Church largely unsullied by Greek philosophy. I have presented just a flavour of their activities and importance and, of course this has not been an unbroken line, though it was interesting to trace a path from Wycliffe in Oxford to Wesley in London, by way of Prague, Bohemia and Moravia.

There are probably many stories yet untold, through lack of historical material, largely thanks to the state-church-sponsored medieval book burnings. But it is fair to say that God has always preserved a faithful remnant, a Church holding on to Biblical principles and living their lives accordingly. And what were these Biblical principles that informed their actions? This is where we are journeying to next, to try and get inside the heads of the very first Christians …

PART TWO

The Truth

Home, James

Now for the real challenging bit. Is it possible to get inside the minds of those first Jewish believers in Jesus? Are we able to discern their thought processes and their motivations? Can we discover how they saw their relationship with each other, with the World around them, with God? How can we honestly do this?

All we have is written words, of which we have two kinds. We have historical documents, some written by tried and tested commentators, others of more dubious origin, still others nothing more than self-supporting propaganda. Then there's Holy Scripture. As Christians, we are in a privileged position, though others would call it a blinkered one. We trust 100% in God's Word; without that trust our faith is in vain. So we can forge ahead in certainty if we are guided by Holy Scripture – correctly interpreted. Only the Bible! *Sola Scriptura!*

Correctly interpreted? The only catch. How many times have you heard a preacher, in the flesh or on TV, claim "The Bible says …", with theatrical certainty, usually wielding the said object as a visual aid? What they are really saying is, *I believe that, in order to prove my argument, the Bible says* ... This is fine and dandy when the preacher is developing his argument from Scripture, correctly applied, rather than using Scripture as a convenient confirmation of his own arguments, regardless of context.

If I am going to develop a picture of these early Jewish Christians, the Bible has to be the bedrock of my argument, the foundation stone of my story. So let me take you back to those exciting, spiritually-charged days, described in the Acts of the Apostles. Specifically we drop in on the events as described in Chapter 15. James, the leader of the Jerusalem church, had wrapped up a crucial meeting on *what to do with the Gentiles* and a letter had been written and delivered to the church at Antioch.

As an aside, isn't it strange that the New Testament name "James" is exactly the same as the Old Testament name, "Jacob". Both are translations of the Hebrew name Ya'acov, yet one sounds very Jewish and the other very British. Perhaps the reason why the New Testament translators used the *British* name was in some way to distance Christians from the *Jewish* Old Testament, reinforcing the idea (actually a feature of the ancient heresy, Marcionism) that the Old Testament is out-of-date, somehow lesser among equals (though of course another reason was to keep King James – he of the KJV – happy).

It seems likely that shortly after this, James sat down at his desk and wrote another letter. This letter was written primarily to Jewish believers in Jesus, now scattered all over the Roman world. We know the letter by his name, *James*, and it is probably the earliest piece of writing in the whole New Testament.

Another aside, isn't it strange that the "Jewish" epistles – of James, Hebrews, Peter and Jude – are shoved to the back of the canon, among the final books of the New Testament. Of course there may be a perfectly good reason for this, but this is just a layperson's observation.

So we have the earliest written Scripture of the Church and it was written to Jewish Christians. Here we have a Jewish mind speaking to other Jewish minds; perhaps this letter will give us an insight as to what made those Jewish minds tick; perhaps the content of the letter will offer some helpful clues. This was no parish newsletter; James needed to unload, as there were some serious issues at stake.

With typical Jewish directness, James gets straight to the point. Acknowledging the persecutions that many were suffering, he asks whether any of them are lacking in wisdom:

> *If any of you lacks wisdom, he should ask God, who gives generously to all without finding fault, and it will be given to him. But when he asks, he must believe and not doubt, because he who doubts is like a wave of the sea, blown and tossed by the wind. That man should not think he will receive anything from the Lord; he is a double-minded man, unstable in all he does.*
> (James 1:5-8)

This is so key to our story, because one of the defining features of the human experience, whether Jew or Gentile, is our desire for wisdom, for knowledge, for understanding. Where does this idea come from? Well, that's easy:

> *And the LORD God commanded the man, "You are free to eat from any tree in the garden; but you must not eat from the tree of the knowledge of good and evil, for when you eat of it you will surely die."*
> (Genesis 2:16-17)

It's back to Eden we go, to the First Man. Adam is told that eating from this tree was a particularly bad thing, with dreadful consequences. Then he gets married and his wife, Eve, has an encounter with the serpent:

> *"You will not surely die," the serpent said to the woman. "For God knows that when you eat of it your eyes will be opened, and you will be like God, knowing good and evil."*
> (Genesis 3:4-5)

The first statement is a lie, a direct contradiction of God's command. But what of the second statement? Would eating from this tree give them knowledge of good and evil and the wisdom needed for using this knowledge, or was this another lie?

Well, they ate the fruit and, immediately ... *the eyes of both of them were opened (vs 7).* So the serpent was right on this account. This was no lie.

And the LORD God said, "The man has now become like one of us, knowing good and evil. He must not be allowed to reach out his hand and take also from the tree of life and eat, and live forever." (Genesis 3:22)

They *had* now become like God, knowing good and evil. This was no lie, either. A burning desire had now entered the heart of man, a desire for knowledge and this was not compatible with their life in the Garden of Eden, so they were banished, kept away from the Tree of Life. The fruit of this tree, guaranteeing everlasting life, would now be unattainable for men and women until that day in the future when the redeemed may partake of it.

Blessed are those who wash their robes, that they may have the right to the tree of life and may go through the gates into the city. (Revelation 22:14)

So, this desire for wisdom in the heart of man (and woman) is a consequence of the Fall.

Returning to our James passage:

If any of you lacks wisdom, he should ask God, who gives generously to all without finding fault, and it will be given to him. But when he asks, he must believe and not doubt, because he who doubts is like a wave of the sea, blown and tossed by the wind. That man should not think he will receive anything from the Lord; he is a double-minded man, unstable in all he does. (James 1:5-8)

James is saying that the search for wisdom is a good thing only when a certain ingredient is present. We should *ask God* for this wisdom, but we must ask with belief, with *faith*. Without faith, there is no point asking as we will always doubt any answer we may get.

This idea is further developed theologically by the intellectual force that is known as Paul, in his letter to the Corinthians:

> *We have not received the spirit of the world but the Spirit who is from God, that we may understand what God has freely given us. This is what we speak, not in words taught us by human wisdom but in words taught by the Spirit, expressing spiritual truths in spiritual words. The man without the Spirit does not accept the things that come from the Spirit of God, for they are foolishness to him, and he cannot understand them, because they are spiritually discerned. The spiritual man makes judgments about all things, but he himself is not subject to any man's judgment: "For who has known the mind of the Lord that he may instruct him?" But we have the mind of Christ.*

(1 Corinthians 2:12-16)

Oh to have the *mind of Christ*, because if we truly can live in this state, then we are going to easily fulfil the task set at the head of this chapter, getting inside the heads of those first believers in Jesus, who surely also had the mind of Christ, as Paul declared.

To achieve this we need the wisdom that comes from God, through faith, not that which comes from the World. James has some harsh words to say about this:

> *Who is wise and understanding among you? Let him show it by his good life, by deeds done in the humility that comes from wisdom. But if you harbour bitter envy and selfish ambition in your hearts, do not boast about it or deny the truth. Such "wisdom" does not come down from heaven but is earthly, unspiritual, of the devil. For where you have envy and selfish ambition, there you*

find disorder and every evil practice. But the wisdom that comes from heaven is first of all pure; then peace-loving, considerate, submissive, full of mercy and good fruit, impartial and sincere. (James 3:13-17)

Let's now pause and regroup. The first feature of the mindset of those first Jewish Christians – assuming they followed the teachings of James and Paul – is their attitude to wisdom. All knowledge, and the wisdom to apply it, was to come from God, through prayer, Scripture and the teaching of the apostles. All other wisdom is from the World or from the devil, producing envy, selfishness, disorder and every evil practice.

What else does James show us through his letter? There is much about doing things. Faith and wisdom are fine, but, when combined with actions, this is where real Christian living kicks in. Here are examples:

Do not merely listen to the word, and so deceive yourselves. Do what it says. Anyone who listens to the word but does not do what it says is like a man who looks at his face in a mirror and, after looking at himself, goes away and immediately forgets what he looks like. But the man who looks intently into the perfect law that gives freedom, and continues to do this, not forgetting what he has heard, but doing it – he will be blessed in what he does. (James 1:22-25)

If you really keep the royal law found in Scripture, "Love your neighbour as yourself," you are doing right. But if you show favouritism, you sin and are convicted by the law as lawbreakers. For whoever keeps the whole law and yet stumbles at just one point is guilty of breaking all of it. For he who said, "Do not commit adultery," also said, "Do not murder." If you do not commit adultery but do commit murder, you have become a lawbreaker. Speak and act as those who are going to be judged by the law that gives freedom, because judgment without mercy will be shown to anyone who has not been merciful. Mercy triumphs over judgment!

(James 2:8-13)

This passage reminds us of a more famous one from the Gospels, *the Sermon on the Mount*, which shows us that, just as in our sound-byte-driven world, where snippets of information fly through the media in its many guises, the writers of Scripture in the 1st Century were drawing from a pool of quotations, teachings and observations. I find that very real and comforting and conjures up an atmosphere of shared excitement and the bursting of a desire to *get the story out.*

The royal law, also known as *the golden rule*, is actually part of the Hebrew Scriptures, from Leviticus:

Do not seek revenge or bear a grudge against one of your people, but love your neighbour as yourself. I am the LORD.
(Leviticus 19:18)

It is then expanded by Jesus in the aforementioned Sermon on the Mount:

You have heard that it was said, 'Love your neighbour and hate your enemy.' But I tell you: Love your enemies and pray for those who persecute you ...
(Matthew 5:43-44)

And, later on, when the Pharisees were trying to tie him up in theological knots, he cleverly undid them.

One of them, an expert in the law, tested him with this question: "Teacher, which is the greatest commandment in the Law?" Jesus replied: " 'Love the Lord your God with all your heart and with all your soul and with all your mind.' This is the first and greatest commandment. And the second is like it: 'Love your

neighbour as yourself.' All the Law and the Prophets hang on these two commandments. "
(Matthew 22:35-40)

In this statement Jesus was simply summarising the Ten Commandments, knocking them down to the bare bones and declaring that they are really just about *love*, primarily for God but also for our fellow man. This is not wishy-washy glassy-eyed sentimentality, this is real, practical, get-your-hands-dirty love, expressed as devotion to the Lord God and also reflected in the way we conduct ourselves with our fellow man.

Love for God is expressed in our worship of Him alone and our respect for His name, by not swearing or blaspheming. Love for our fellow man, our neighbour, is expressed in honouring our parents and not to murder, sleep around, steal, lie or covet.

These are all external actions, or, in the words of James, one's *deeds*.

What good is it, my brothers, if a man claims to have faith but has no deeds? Can such faith save him?
(James 2:14)

So it's back to James' letter to the Jewish Christians, dispersed throughout the Roman world. We have seen the importance of wisdom, but learned that without faith it is useless. Now we see that faith is also useless without deeds. James says it even more strongly ...

As the body without the spirit is dead, so faith without deeds is dead.
(James 2:26)

Faith is the common factor, as well it should be, because faith is our lifeline, our connection to God. Without faith we're swinging aimlessly over an abyss, without a hope in the World.

So faith in God underpins our wisdom, which compels us
to perform our deeds.

Here's where we are. We have distilled a central message of the letter
from James to the early Jewish believers in Jesus. The centrality
of faith is evident, both in how we process the information that
bombards us daily and how we convert it into action.

How have individual churches fared against this plumb-line?
Have they always acted with godly wisdom? Let's comb the pages
of history and look for evidence.

The very first Church of Acts was a Jewish Church. If there
was one thing about the Jews of that day, it was that God was
a given. There was too much history (chronicled warts-and-all
in the pages of the Old Testament) between the people and their
Deity for the lack of faith to be an issue. God and His people
were very much an item, although these particular people were
blinkered, as a whole, when it came to the earthly visitation of
the *Son* of God and all that entailed. So it stood to reason that
those Jews who *had* accepted Jesus as the Son of God and who
had arranged themselves in those first churches, were wise in the
ways of God.

So what evidence do we have that these Jewish Christians were
walking and acting with godly wisdom? First we look at how James
described this state of being:

But the wisdom that comes from heaven is first of all pure; then
peace-loving, considerate, submissive, full of mercy and good
fruit, impartial and sincere.
(James 3:17)

And the wisdom that is unacceptable?

But if you harbour bitter envy and selfish ambition in your hearts,
do not boast about it or deny the truth. Such "wisdom" does not
come down from heaven but is earthly, unspiritual, of the devil.

*For where you have envy and selfish ambition, there you find
disorder and every evil practice.*
(James 3:14-16)

He summarises it so:

*Who is wise and understanding among you? Let him show
it by his good life, by deeds done in the humility that comes
from wisdom.*
(James 3:13)

So we look through the early chapters of the Book of Acts and
decide whether those Christians generally acted in a peace-loving,
considerate, submissive, merciful, impartial and sincere way or
whether they were motivated by envy and selfish ambition.

We do not have reams of information in the Biblical account, but
what we have tends to tell a story that these people were acting out
of godly wisdom, as imparted by the apostles and teachers:

*They devoted themselves to the apostles' teaching and to the
fellowship, to the breaking of bread and to prayer. Everyone
was filled with awe, and many wonders and miraculous signs
were done by the apostles. All the believers were together
and had everything in common. Selling their possessions
and goods, they gave to anyone as he had need. Every day
they continued to meet together in the temple courts. They
broke bread in their homes and ate together with glad and
sincere hearts, praising God and enjoying the favour of all
the people. And the Lord added to their number daily those
who were being saved.*
(Acts 2:42-47)

Of course nobody's perfect and the apostles Paul, Peter and John
wouldn't have felt it necessary to add a few rebukes and corrections
in their letters if everyone had got it right. John felt it necessary

to say a few words about specific churches and their shortcoming
before getting into the nitty-gritty of the Revelation.

When we move forwards to the next chapter of Church history
we encounter a significant development. *Other ideas* were seeping
into the Church, through the writings and teachings of the Church
Fathers, pagan ideas from the Greek philosophers. Paul saw
it coming:

> *See to it that no one takes you captive through hollow and*
> *deceptive philosophy, which depends on human tradition and the*
> *basic principles of this world rather than on Christ.*
> (Colossians 2:8)

Those who have followed the story of this pagan infiltration through
my last two books can guess what's coming next! Here is a short
review of the damage done to the pure gospel of Jesus Christ.

Plato introduced the idea of *dualism* into the Church, the idea that
the physical universe/nature is bad and the spiritual universe/nature
is good. Out of this came a whole menagerie of cults and heresies,
some still with us today and even present within the thinking of
some mainstream denominations. Plato's tentacles are far reaching
and adaptive, affecting our view of God and Jesus, the way that we
worship and particularly the way we interpret Holy Scripture.

Aristotle seemed harmless, even a positive influence. *After all,*
didn't he just encourage us to think? He did, but he tempted us
into thinking dangerous thoughts. The blame was not on him, after
all he never claimed to have godly wisdom, but those Christian
philosophers and leaders of the medieval Church who claimed
divine license, felt free to allow these dangerous thoughts to break
through the shackles of godly wisdom. It was now acceptable to use
our rational minds to analyse and dissect the Word of God, without
any acknowledgement that Holy Scripture is, first and foremost,
God's revealed word to mankind.

Plato, through the teaching of Augustine, introduced such
deviations as the clergy/laity divide and Church hierarchies. It also

gave licence, through the use of allegory and the 'spiritualisation' of the text, for teachers to read their own ideas and prejudices into their interpretation of Holy Scripture, relegating God to the role of rubber-stamper for such aberrations as antisemitism, persecution of 'other' Christians, religious war, slavery and prejudice against women.

The influence of Aristotle, largely through the teachings of Thomas Aquinas, led to a Christianity that was man-centred, driven by rationalism, rather than God-centred, underpinned by faith in God. What started out as a synthesis of faith and reason, led to the gradual loosening of God's certainties on the human heart, affecting doctrines and practices and producing a faith diluted through compromise.

Hopefully you can see where all this is leading. It's not rocket-science to see that, in terms of our plumb-line statement at the head of the chapter, we have moved on to pastures new, or should I say uncertain terrain, fraught with hidden dangers.

Faith in God underpins our wisdom, which compels us to perform our deeds.

What wisdom, do you think, produced such deeds as the bloody Crusades (did God really expect His people to shed blood in reclaiming a piece of real estate that didn't belong to them anyway?), the Inquisition, book burnings, burning of martyrs (other Christians who differed in matters of doctrine), the mass slaughter of Jews, Waldenses and any other dissident group, the banning of Bibles for the common people, the promotion of non-Biblical aberrations such as the selling of indulgences, the acquisition of vast riches by the State Church while the people went hungry, endless wars between Catholics and Protestants, with atrocities carried out by both sides etc. etc. This list could be made a lot longer, but I believe the point has been made.

Was this all godly wisdom, the result of sincere prayer and the diligent reading of God's Word? Were they acting in a peace-loving, considerate, submissive, merciful, impartial and sincere way or were they motivated by envy and selfish ambition, to say nothing of the promptings of the devil?

Of course this is not a sweeping denunciation of the whole Church since the 2ⁿᵈ Century. It is simply a statement that, since Greek ideas were allowed to infiltrate the Church and to create breaches allowing the devil and the World to enter, it's very hard to see godly wisdom being the only motivation. In fact James has more to say about this:

> *You adulterous people, don't you know that friendship with the world is hatred toward God? Anyone who chooses to be a friend of the world becomes an enemy of God.*
> (James 4:4)

When the Church has become a national entity, integrated with all aspects of secular as well as religious society (even when its influence is largely benign), rather than a network of "called out ones" hasn't it become a friend of the World, with the corresponding penalties? Think about it!

So how does this affect us today? Isn't the Church of today different? Hasn't it learned from past mistakes? Think again!

The Church today, all 38,000 denominations of it, is simply the upper branches of a great tree that was planted in the 1ˢᵗ Century and, since the 2ⁿᵈ Century has been slowly strangled by alien vines and creepers. Some early branches had grown untouched, but most of these, apart from a few notable exceptions, were destroyed.

We still belong to that original tree, we share the same roots, even if the original roots have largely withered through neglect. And it is those original roots that we are going to turn to now, as we tie everything together in the next chapter.

A Tale of
Two Mindsets

This has been a slow unveiling of a sad reality in the Christian Church. It's fairly clear that by-and-large the Western Church of today is at best a distant cousin to the Church of those first apostles. There has been so much baggage added to its sturdy young bones over the last 2,000 years, that now it is creaking to stay upright.

Can we ever get back to how it was in those *halcyon days* (if you excuse my Greek reference)? Is there a possibility of return to our first love or has too much murky water flowed under the bridge? Given that, unlike any other field of human endeavour, we have arguably ended up far worse off than when we started. Is the process of history reversible?

Although many have tried and many have failed, I believe we shouldn't give up trying. In terms of understanding the processes of history, we are possibly better equipped to do so than any of our predecessors. We have unprecedented access to both the official and *unauthorised* accounts of Church history. I can say that, without a shadow of doubt, this book could not have been written without the research and communication possibilities opened up through the Internet.

This is not to say that the task is an easy one, but it could be an interesting one, certainly a challenging one.

Here's the situation as it presents itself to us soon after the start of the 21ˢᵗ Century AD.

◊ Nearly 2,000 years ago there was born a new movement of God like none before or after. It has provided us with a template of the best that there has ever been and we are assured of its authenticity because this first Church lived out its life within the pages of Holy Scripture.

◊ We need to know whether this Church was a one-off unique Church or whether it is possible for us to replicate from that template.

◊ Has Greek thinking, introduced to this Church after the times of the first apostles become too integrated and absorbed into the Body of Christ to make our task possible?

◊ Some have said that God poured out unprecedented gifts and favour to that first Church in order to establish the Christian faith in the hostile Roman world of that day. They add that such gifts and favour are no longer available to the Church.

◊ Despite this, history is dotted with expressions of Christianity that seemed to be free of Greek influences, thrived in Biblical expressions of their faith, even experiencing the miraculous. Were they exceptions or should they be viewed as the possible norm that we should aspire to?

◊ Can a Church survive in the modern age without compromising Biblical principles, where all of our wisdom and deeds are informed by an unswerving faith in God?

So is there a key to unlock the door to such exciting possibilities?

Those of you who have read the previous two books would have detected a single theme running through the narrative, that of two mindsets, each fighting for control of our will. It is time you were formally introduced.

Making the introduction is not a modern theologian, schooled in Jewish hermeneutics and eager to promote understandings of the Hebraic root of Christianity. Instead I pass you over to a 19th Century English cultural commentator, Matthew Arnold, quoting from his essay, *Culture and Anarchy*.

We show, as a nation, a great energy and persistence in walking according to the best light we have. We may regard this energy, this obligation of duty, self-control, and work as one force. And we may regard the intelligence driving at those ideas, the indomitable impulse to know and adjust them perfectly, as another force. And these two forces we may regard as in some sense rivals, as exhibited in man and his history and rivals dividing the empire of the world between them. And to give these forces names from the two races of men who have supplied the most signal and splendid manifestations of them, we may call them respectively the forces of Hebraism and Hellenism. Hebraism and Hellenism, between these two points of influence moves our world.

Hebraism and Hellenism or, in slightly more modern terms, *Hebraic thought* and *Greek thought*.

He has introduced these mindsets in a truly grand manner, as if they are the only true motivations that mankind has. This is a bold statement to make, but is it true?

I believe this is probably true; I believe this is important; I believe that every Christian needs to grasp this simple truth and I will spend the rest of this chapter explaining why, and the rest of this book showing how!

Let's first see how Arnold introduced them. Hebraic thought is bound up in *obligation of duty and self-control*, whereas Greek thought is characterised by *the indomitable impulse to know and adjust the ideas of man.*

Arnold continues:

> *The uppermost idea with Hellenism is to see things as they really are; the uppermost idea with Hebraism is conduct and obedience ... the Greek quarrel with the body and its desires is that they hinder right thinking, the Hebrew quarrel with them is that they hinder right acting.*

So first impressions are that Greek thought is bound up in *thinking about things,* whereas Hebraic thought is all about *doing things the right way.*

Let's pause and consider this rather simplistic definition. In fact let's have a wander around the garden while we are doing so; let's return to the Garden of Eden.

> *And the LORD God commanded the man, "You are free to eat from any tree in the garden; but you must not eat from the tree of the knowledge of good and evil, for when you eat of it you will surely die."*
> (Genesis 2:16-17)

Before Adam fell from grace he was quite a busy boy. He had started his reign as King over the animals, birds and fish with the specific job of naming them. After he fell from grace the first thing he did was to realise that he was naked and out of that thought came two actions, the procuring of underwear and a sudden fear of God. Yet Adam and Eve were naked before they had eaten the forbidden fruit and had felt neither shame nor fear then. What was the difference? The difference was that they now, in some mysterious way, had knowledge of good and evil and had woken up to the inner life of the mind, with new ideas about their state of undress. Ask yourself this – *where did this new knowledge come from?* It wasn't from God or the snake, otherwise we would have been told so. It was from their own reasoning. We, too, have inherited this new trait; it is part of what we are as fallen creatures.

It's almost as if ... and I confess I am making a jump here, but please indulge me ... the default state for man (and woman) since the fall is a propensity to *think about things*, to procrastinate, to rationalise. This would contrast with the default state of Adam before his fall as one who *did things*. Could this mean that the *Hebraic* mindset was the original default and the *Greek* mindset is the new default? Before you totally dismiss my imaginings, just hold these ideas in mind until I return to them shortly.

Let's go back to our 19th Century friend, as he develops his argument:

The governing idea of Hellenism is spontaneity of consciousness; that of Hebraism, strictness of conscience. Christianity changed nothing in this essential bent of Hebraism to set doing above knowing. Self-conquest, self-devotion, the following not our own individual will, but the will of God, obedience, is the fundamental idea of this form, also, of the discipline to which we have attached the general name of Hebraism.

So Arnold equates Christianity, with its accent on obedience to the will of God, with Hebraism. One further quote from him to really seal the deal on this:

As Hellenism speaks of thinking clearly, seeing things in their essence and beauty, as a grand and precious feat for man to achieve, so Hebraism speaks of becoming conscious of sin, of awakening to a sense of sin, as a feat of this kind. It is obvious to what wide divergence these differing tendencies, actively followed, must lead.

This is a tale of two mindsets. We may call them the Hebraic and Greek mindsets or perhaps it would be more helpful and less partisan to strip out the ethnic labels and call them the *Biblical* and *Worldly* mindsets. There are two very good reasons to do so:

◊ They explain, in general terms, where these mindsets come from:

> *You adulterous people, don't you know that friendship with the world is hatred toward God? Anyone who chooses to be a friend of the world becomes an enemy of God. Or do you think Scripture says without reason that the spirit he caused to live in us envies intensely?*
> (James 4:4-5)

◊ We don't unconsciously (and wrongly) associate the mindsets with ethnic groups otherwise we could be in danger of putting Jews on a pedestal and burying Greeks in the foundation of the pedestal.

Yet, on the other hand, the *Greek* and *Hebrew* labels are useful and there are two good reasons for this too.

◊ They identify with the group most associated with the mindset.

◊ They are the terms most often used for the mindsets (e.g. the Matthew Arnold essay, my previous two books and elsewhere).

For the latter reasons I will continue to use these terms.

It is time for a cross-over. By now – especially if you have read the previous two books in this series – you should be thoroughly acquainted with the Greek mindset. I have probably analysed it to death. I have allowed my own natural-born Greek mindset to pull itself to pieces and lay it bare for all to see. It is time to move on.

The Hebrew (or Hebraic) mindset. What *exactly* is it?

We start with Matthew Arnold. He called it the obligation of duty, self-control, conduct and obedience, right acting, strictness of conscience, following the will of God and becoming conscious of sin.

What does this remind one of? Our response to *the Gospel*, which is not surprising, as the Gospel of Jesus Christ came from a

Hebraic mindset, from Hebrew thinking, as we already read from Arnold's essay.

Remember what we concluded in Chapter Five, from looking at the Golden Rule, the Sermon of the Mount and the Book of James.

Faith in God underpins our wisdom, which compels us to perform our deeds.

This is Hebrew thinking, the Hebraic mindset. The key to the Hebraic mindset is faith in God and the result of the Hebraic mindset is the performing of deeds.

Faith and works, they are at the heart of our Christian faith, our *Hebraic* Christian faith.

Now this ain't brain surgery. For many of you I am stating the obvious but perhaps it needs to be stated and re-stated and re-re-stated.

Faith and works. Let's remind ourselves what James had to say:

Do not merely listen to the word, and so deceive yourselves. Do what it says. Anyone who listens to the word but does not do what it says is like a man who looks at his face in a mirror and, after looking at himself, goes away and immediately forgets what he looks like. But the man who looks intently into the perfect law that gives freedom, and continues to do this, not forgetting what he has heard, but doing it – he will be blessed in what he does. (James 1:22-25)

Let's be honest, how many Christians do we know who have all the theory, can recite creeds and liturgies, but walk around with a scowl / frown / superior smirk and would no more put themselves out for someone than entertain a few bum notes by the worship group?

This will be driven home when we look at the following series of contrasts between Hebraic thinking and Greek thinking, in the way we understand God and His ways. Then we must seriously consider where we put our personal priorities.

◊ The Greek mind says that man is at the centre of life; the Hebraic mind says that God is at the centre of life.

◊ The Greek mind says that the things of God must be deduced from our logical minds; the Hebraic mind says that the things of God can only be understood by faith and revelation.

◊ The Greek mind says that we should strive for knowledge *about* God; the Hebraic mind says that we should *know* God.

These are just words and concepts. We need to let them really sink in and soak us in their truths. It may take time, but it will be worth it. Just think of that last one again. I will repeat it.

The Greek mind says that we should strive for knowledge about God; the Hebraic mind says that we should know God.

Think about it. The Greek part of us inclines us towards building ourselves a whole library of books, podcasts and sermons that help to build up a systematic theology of God, an understanding of His attributes. The Hebraic part of us inclines us to drop to our knees and ask Him to teach us His ways. The Greek part of us inclines us to read Bible commentaries, benefiting from the wisdom of scholars. The Hebraic part of us inclines us to read the Bible alone and pray for revelation and illumination.

There's another way to look at the differences. It was said that Socrates, the acknowledged mighty man of Greek philosophy, had a unique way of thinking through problems. He just stood still for ages in deep thought until the solution presented itself. This couldn't be more different to an Orthodox Jew, listening to the reading of Scripture, or deep in prayer. He would rarely keep still, swaying his body to and fro, *davenning* it is called, an expression of devotion to Almighty God. The Greek way is of stillness, rest, self-control; the Hebraic way is of movement, emotion, power, life.

We can go further. The Hebraic and Greek mindsets can be summarised in single words. The Greek way is the way of *man*, but the Hebraic way is the Biblical way, is the Christian way, is the way of *God*. We *all* become Hebraic at the point of conversion, this wonderful *New Creation* when God in the person of the Holy Spirit comes into our lives, but the World drags us back to our Greek ways, the way of *man*, to the degree that we allow it to.

The truth is in plain sight, but perhaps we have lost it. The Christian faith is not about man at all, it is about God. It is His initiative. God chooses us to become His people. The goal of sanctification is to *become like Jesus* in this life; the goal of justification is *to be with God* in the next life!

This is the ideal we must all strive for, but sometimes we lose sight of it. Perhaps we have forgotten how to strive for it. In the next chapter we will consider this as we start to move from theory to practice.

Rewiring the Brain

This has got to be one of the hardest chapters I have ever had to write. I am suggesting that ideally we need to install a new operating system and then reboot our brains. Knowing that this is impossible, I am then going to further suggest that a more reasonable approach is an incremental one, a gradual process to encourage us to think more as God would want us to and less as the World has trained us to.

The problem is that the Western mind, certainly for the last few hundred years or so, has been taught to think in a certain way, a Greek way. This hasn't always done us much harm as it has enabled all of the scientific advances that make life so comfortable and safe for us. But of course there has also been a flip side, a darker side of technological advances in warfare, population control and such infringements. Greek thinking, the deductive and empirical reasoning that flowed particularly from the writings of Aristotle, has provided us with a form of human progress, though it has come at a cost. It has provided us with safety and comfort and convenient living, but it has taken us away from our relationship with God, who surely provides a better way.

Here's the problem. This Greek mindset, encouraging us to rely on brainpower to think everything through, is totally unsuitable for discerning the ways of God. And since the goal of every Christian is to discern God's ways for his/her life, we have ended up with an imbalance.

God's revelation to us, His Holy Scripture, was written on His behalf by people who operated in the Hebraic mindset, a way of thinking that put God at the centre. And, just as you wouldn't use a Spanish dictionary to translate from Italian into English, the Greek mindset isn't the best tool to use to feed one's soul with God's instructions. So here we are, a folk who have learned to think in a certain logical, deductive, Greek way since our schooldays, encountering a Book that will only fully reveal its secrets to those who are trained to read it.

What I am *not* saying is that we can't read the Bible and get great joy, assurance and instruction from doing so. But what I *am* saying is that we probably miss out on much and certainly get some things wrong if we are not using the right tools.

I've said this before, but I will repeat it, the people who first possessed the Hebraic mindset, the Jews from Bible times, were trained from early childhood to think this way. Scripture was fed into their minds and spirits as soon as they were on solid food, in much the same way as we do with "reality" TV and celebrity gossip. By teenage years, The Torah was memorised in much the same way as song lyrics and celebrity biographic details are by today's youth. The ways of God came naturally (even if they weren't always followed) just as our current insatiable appetite for the ways of whatever men or women are being currently blogged or tweeted about come naturally.

Do you really think God considers it the ideal situation for us to engage with Him with just the small part of our mind uncluttered with nonsense and trivia? Yes, this sounds very old-fogey-ish, but one of the first things we must train our minds to do, if we want to start thinking Hebraically, is to say to ourselves, *what would God think about this?* We have to switch perspectives and learn to think, speak and act accordingly. And, boy, this ain't easy!

Before we go any further this is a good place to address the one thought that may be troubling you over this *Hebraic* thing.

Isn't this a Jewish thing? I've heard of the Hebrew Roots
movement – doesn't this mean that we are obliged to
keep the Sabbath and the Jewish festivals, eat kosher,
wear a kippah, speak Yiddish and learn some acceptable
Jewish jokes?

This is the common perception ... and it is wrong ... mostly.

The Hebrew Roots movement started as a sincere and welcome desire to explore the Jewish roots of Christianity and *see where that leads.* It has led to many ways – some good, some bad and some dangerous. In many cases it has led to division and spiritual arrogance; in other cases it has been a real enrichment and a rekindling of a desire to go deeper into the things of God. It is not my intention here to analyse this further except to say that this is *not* what I mean by the Hebraic mindset.

The Hebraic mindset is a way of thinking and exploring the consequences. It is not purely a way of acting, particularly if these actions just lead to confusion, resentment and a blurring around the edges between Jew and Gentile. The Hebraic mindset has been demonstrated in history by Christians who couldn't tell the difference between a menorah and a fedora and there are many within the current Hebrew Roots movement who are more Greek in their thinking than the current Pope!

Being Hebraic is not necessarily celebrating the Sabbath and the Jewish festivals, or wearing a *kippah* or a *tallit*, or speaking Yiddish/Hebrew, or supporting Israel, or going to a Messianic Fellowship. These can all be the result of a Hebraic mindset (correctly applied), but not necessarily. These are all external actions and, unless they are prompted by a sincere Hebraic heart, then they are just observances. Similarly, being Hebraic does not mean that you *have to* celebrate the Sabbath and/or Jewish holidays or wear a kippah or tallit or have to speak Yiddish or Hebrew or have to support Israel or have to go to a Messianic Fellowship.

So let's not get confused. Let us focus on the internal, on what is at the root of our thinking and motivations. Let's summarise what we have learned so far about the Hebraic mindset:

◊ Putting God at the centre of what we do.

◊ Exercising faith in God.

◊ Actions resulting from this faith.

This can be refined into three areas:

◊ Living Hebraically – God centred lives.

◊ Thinking Hebraically – thoughts driven by faith in God.

◊ Acting Hebraically – actions inspired by faith in God.

How much of our Christianity is 'man-centred' rather than 'God-centred', however much we may deny it? Let's return again to the Garden of Eden.

I suggested that perhaps the Hebraic, "God-centred", mindset was the default before Adam sinned and the Greek mindset became the default after he sinned. You can't deny that the focus did shift as a result of the fall, from God to man. The original state found Adam and Eve in communion with God, following His instructions and living in a God-created Paradise. The fallen state, however, saw Adam and Eve acting on their own initiative, disobeying God and forced to leave the Paradise and create a life for themselves. This is what we have inherited and perhaps it is fair to say that, despite all of the scientific progress that man has made, our yearning is nothing more than to return to the simplicity and connectedness of the Garden of Eden. I contend that this is the goal of the Hebraic mind.

So, theory into practice. How do we move forwards?

We can first have a fresh but serious look at some current

Christian practices and ask ourselves the question, has this been prompted by God or man?

Fundraising, campaigns and initiatives, prophetic utterances, accountability, quiche, use of God's name, manipulation of Holy Spirit, re-imagining Jesus, The Bible says ..., attitudes to Jews and other Christian groups, ecumenicalism, liberation theology, worship songs, management and marketing techniques ...

An interesting mix? Some of them quite major issues, others veering toward triviality, yet all worthy of investigation. Many of these areas and more are going to be discussed in the next section. In all of our discussions we are going to look objectively at the issue, try to ascertain how the issue reflects on the mindset behind it and do our best to ask the question, *has this been prompted by God or man?*

How Hebraic or Greek is the Church today? I would suggest that every church, whether individual congregation or multi-national denomination, has elements of both. A rough guide would be to look at four church types:

Word: those churches that emphasise the written Word of God e.g. Reformed Churches.

Spirit: those churches that emphasise the work of the Holy Spirit e.g. Charismatic Churches.

Tradition: those churches that emphasise a handed-down tradition e.g. Catholic Church, Anglican Church.

World: those churches that emphasise engagement with the World e.g. Emergent Church.

The Hebraic, *God-centred*, mindset would feature mainly in the first two. The Greek, *man-centred*, mindset would feature mainly in the last two.

Where does your church fit in? It probably would fit broadly in one or two of the above types, but it would probably have elements of the others, too.

We must also seriously consider our attitude and use of the Bible, God's Word. If we have been using Greek rationalism and deductive thinking to discern what God is telling us through His Word, then what other ways are there? How does the Hebraic mindset read the Bible?

This question has been answered, albeit fairly briefly, in the previous two books and is a huge subject. So rather than repeating myself yet again, this issue will be dealt with as it becomes relevant to the narrative. That way we will be teasing out God's meanings from the text in a natural manner, rather than battering you with yet more theory, which you would have forgotten by the time that we actually need to use it.

Interestingly, this is how the Bible ought to be used. It is called *exegesis* and it is rather exciting. It treats the Bible as a living entity rather than the dry tome that many imagine it to be.

The Bible is not just a collection of words for life; it is life itself. In the next section we are going to use this wonderful gift of God to re-examine key areas of our Christian life. Using the *Hebraic* mindset, we will prod gently, maybe not so gently in some areas. There may be some surprises, though there will also be many affirmations. Condemnations are not intended though there are no apologies for highlighting and correcting areas where traditions and the World have somewhat blurred the truth. There may just be the need for some tweaking and slight adjustments. On the other hand you may choose to disagree with my conclusions, which is fine. Let Paul set the tone for our wanderings:

Finally, brothers, whatever is true, whatever is noble, whatever is right, whatever is pure, whatever is lovely, whatever is admirable – if anything is excellent or praiseworthy – think about such things.
(Philippians 4:8)

Oh, what interesting places we are going to explore together in the next section …

Observation #1: Ten Greek things some Christians do …

Just a bit of serious fun, but have a look at this list. Do you know anyone guilty of some or all of these? This is not a condemnation, just an observation. This is a taster for the next section, where we will discuss these issues further.

1. **Fall out with each other over minor matters of doctrine** – Christian unity is a precious thing and not to be sacrificed on the altar of cleverness.

2. **Argue endlessly with atheists** – The Christian faith is about relationship with Jesus, not an arena for intellectual debate, as only the Holy Spirit is going to convict souls.

3. **Are able to justify just about anything from the Bible** – Allegory and the 'spiritualising' of Bible text are rife these days with 'teachers' twisting Scripture to support their ideas or questionable behaviour.

4. **Consider that Church is what you do on Sunday mornings** – The church is not the building, but the people who meet inside it, who also exist the rest of the week outside the building!

5. **Believe that the Jewish people are rejected by God** – The roots of this idea are firmly within ideas from Greek philosophy.

6. **Listen to a sermon uncritically** – We are urged to be like the Bereans, who measured the words of Paul against Holy Scripture and were not afraid to challenge the preacher.

7. **Have a high view of Church traditions** – There is no higher authority for a Christian than the written words of God, Holy Scripture. Church traditions should never have a higher place.

8. **Refuse to visit churches of a different denomination** – We are the Body of Christ. The fact that we meet in different places and

follow different means of expressing our faith should not stop us from meeting each other.

9. **Believe that drums are the tools of the devil** – Joy in worship is a wonderful thing. Just because some instruments have been put to profane use should not stop us from using them to worship God.

10. **Eat quiche** – Can't stand the stuff. There must be some sort of Greek angle I can use to vilify this horrible concoction!

PART THREE

The Life

Big Father

Life in London is like experiencing the Big Brother house, without the certainty of an eventual escape into freedom. CCTV cameras follow us everywhere, all communications are monitored in one way or another and all of our transactions are electronically traced. It is sold to us under the pretext of the war against terror. It has instead provided us with an edgy existence, with freedoms leaking away at an ever-increasing rate and hard-won personal liberties slyly chipped away while we are not looking. The people watching and monitoring you and me are ordinary folk like you and me, servants of the state, who are probably themselves closely monitored by another level of public servants. And so it goes on, a self-feeding mechanism guided by no absolute moral or ethical code save that of *the ends justifying the means.*

Thank goodness we have a *Big Father* who does similarly, but with very different objectives in mind.

Consider the ravens: They do not sow or reap, they have no storeroom or barn; yet God feeds them. And how much more valuable you are than birds!
(Luke 12:24)

To the State we are a social security number, to banks we are an account number, to Inland Revenue a tax reference number, but God incredibly sees us as individuals, valuable and important to Him. To the State we are worker ants, to God we are all Queen Bees.

There's another difference. We only come to the attention of the State when we become a statistic, when a parent fills out a birth certificate. God has known us a bit longer than that.

For you created my inmost being; you knit me together in my mother's womb. I praise you because I am fearfully and wonderfully made; your works are wonderful, I know that full well. My frame was not hidden from you when I was made in the secret place. When I was woven together in the depths of the earth, your eyes saw my unformed body. All the days ordained for me were written in your book before one of them came to be.
(Psalm 139:13-16)

He knew when we would be born and He already knows when we're going to die. What happens between those points is up to us, but He's still very much involved.

Question: If we Christians know that God constantly watches over us, why do we still act as if He doesn't?

Jonah and Adam thought they could hide from God's presence, but that same Psalm tells us otherwise.

Where can I go from your Spirit? Where can I flee from your presence? If I go up to the heavens, you are there; if I make my bed in the depths, you are there. If I rise on the wings of the dawn, if I settle on the far side of the sea, even there your hand will guide me, your right hand will hold me fast.
(Psalm 139:7-10)

Let's face it, our dealings with God are usually on our terms, from our own perspective of living from day to day.

Having said that, let's review what we learned in the last section about the two mindsets. The Greek mindset puts *man* at the centre of things, the Hebraic mindset puts *God* there. So, where have we laid our hats? Where have you laid your hat?

If God is *always* at the centre of our thinking then *all* of our thoughts and actions should be designed to please Him. This includes our thoughts and actions when others aren't looking, our thoughts and actions when we are outside human radar, when we are lying in our beds, when we are feeding our minds and spirits with questionable material from our TVs, radios, mp3s and computers. There is no toggle switch between the Holy Spirit and our own, the connection is only impaired when we have clogged things up. How can you be sure that God is pleased with the data stream that is your daily life?

But the eyes of the Lord are on those who fear him, on those whose hope is in his unfailing love ...
(Psalm 33:18)

For the eyes of the Lord range throughout the earth to strengthen those whose hearts are fully committed to him ...
(2 Chronicles 16:9)

Of course no-one's perfect and we're all bound for failure in one sense or another, so we are eternally grateful for the provision of repentance and forgiveness. But how conscious are we of every sin we have committed? The big ones tend to screw up the conscience so much that we are forced to act to put things right or at least to acknowledge the situation. But some of the smaller ones may not be picked up by the conscience filter, because we've taken our eyes off God or have become so wrapped up in ourselves. These accumulate and can form little mounds of spiritual filth, serving no purpose other than to obscure the face of God in our lives.

For the wages of sin is death ...
(Romans 6:23)

If we are honest, how many of us can admit there are some sins we knowingly commit again and again, secure in the knowledge that forgiveness and restoration is available *after the act*? Is this abuse of the system, invoking the letter of the law but diminishing the incredible provision of grace that God has made available to us at such great cost?

It is the mindset of *cheap grace*, where God's free gift to us has become a commodity, the currency of forgiveness, a mechanism that we can unthinkingly and mechanically invoke. If it has just come down to a formula, where we say a prayer of repentance, then instant repentance kicks in and we're free to sin again, then something's very wrong.

The German theologian, Dietrich Bonhoeffer, called it *"the preaching of forgiveness without requiring repentance, baptism without church discipline. Communion without confession. Cheap grace is grace without discipleship, grace without the cross, grace without Jesus Christ."*

As I said, it's a mindset. It's about relationship with God, not formulae or systems. Otherwise, how different are we from the Jews in the Old Testament, to whom the Psalmist says:

> *You do not delight in sacrifice, or I would bring it; you do not take pleasure in burnt offerings. The sacrifices of God are a broken spirit; a broken and contrite heart, O God, you will not despise.*
> (Psalm 51:16-17)

It's the same mindset used by the Catholic church, which has created a complex man-made system dealing with sins, substituting the *Hebraic* relationship between a believer and their God with a hierarchical *Greek* system involving confessionals, indulgences, rosaries and pious exercises.

There is a carnality that has crept into the Church that has diminished, even trivialised, the system that God has put in place for us to ensure that we are walking the walk as God has intended. If we were truly living 100% for God, then surely we wouldn't be looking for loopholes or burying our head in the sand. Instead we would put Him first, *always*. That is the Hebraic way.

So is there anything we could be doing that we're not doing now?

Here's a good place to start.

Do not conform any longer to the pattern of this world, but be transformed by the renewing of your mind. Then you will be able to test and approve what God's will is – his good, pleasing and perfect will.
(Romans 12:2)

We need to be driven by the will of God for our lives, not the pattern imposed on us by the World. Let's see how some Bible folk did it.

What connected Abel, Enoch, Noah, Abraham, Isaac, Jacob, Joseph, Moses (and his parents), Rahab the prostitute, Gideon, Barak, Samson, Jephthah, David, Samuel and the rest of the Old Testament prophets? One word – *faith* – in God, as described in Hebrews 11.

These were all commended for their faith, yet none of them received what had been promised. God had planned something better for us so that only together with us would they be made perfect.
(Hebrews 11:39-40)

Each of these people acted at least once in their lives, usually at great cost, in response to a command from an invisible God, whether it was building an ark, leaving a comfortable home or becoming a national leader. Each took a risk, sacrificing pride or comfort or a quiet life for a walk with the invisible Lord God, despite the very real possibility of danger. God was able to do mighty things through these folk and we read and are inspired by their stories, woven as they are into the narrative of Holy Scripture. The story is much the same in the New Testament. Men put God first, often making the ultimate sacrifice – after the example set by Jesus himself – in order for the Gospel to be preached to all. None of the first apostles lived in comfort and prosperity to a ripe old age; God was the centre of their motivation, not personal ambition or fulfilment.

Then came the Church age and, as explained in my previous book (How the Church lost The Truth), two new factors came into play, both subtly inspired by ideas from Greek philosophy. From the *dualism* of Plato, dividing up the clergy and laity, the "spiritual" people and the hoi-polloi, came the corruption of State Christianity, with *the Church* replacing Jesus as the means for salvation, through the rules and regulations of the sacramental system.

As a reaction to this came the Protestant Reformation, emphasising the individual's own responsibility for his salvation. Although this was a welcome return to Biblical certainties, the Protestants too had their State Churches. They weren't quite "the new broom sweeping all clean" that many think them to be, because they shared with the Catholics an admiration for Augustine, the Plato-inspired Christian philosopher, who created the theological basis for State Churches. Hence the great hierarchies of the Lutherans, Church of England and others.

But, there was worse to come and this was when the *rationalism* of the Greek philosopher Aristotle was stirred into the Christian mix by Thomas Aquinas and developed into a kind of Christian humanism that has made inroads into every expression of Protestant and evangelical Christianity right up to the current day. This was a gradual replacing of God with man, as the centre of our Christian life.

To repeat my much used phrase, *the Greek mind says that we should strive for knowledge about God. The Hebrew mind says that we should know God.*

It is clear that the dominant Christian position today, whether you are Catholic, liberal, evangelical, charismatic or even Messianic, is the *Greek one,* the position that puts *us* first, our needs, our cleverness, our aspirations and desires. We develop systematic theologies, coloured of course by our theological persuasions. We generate hundreds of books every week, on the theme of analysing some aspect of God, or suggesting some new programme or formula for finding self-fulfilment through Biblical principles. Here are some recent titles: *What would Jesus eat?*; *10 ways every Woman can sparkle; The Millionaire from Nazareth: His Prosperity Secrets for you.*

The Hebraic mind says that we should *know* God. Simple. It's about *relationship*, not *analysis*. God is a living spiritual Being, who just happens to be the Lord of the Universe, not a faceless entity to be tweaked by our analytical tweezers. Let's face it, how often do we refer to the Holy Spirit as a He, an actual personality, rather than tending to label Him as a kind of impersonal force? Star Wars has a lot to answer for!

Just because God has a personality doesn't mean that He has to play by our rules. He is, after all, the Creator of the Universe, which sort of exempts Him from human rules of etiquette and acceptable behaviour. Sometimes we should just accept the plain truth, that there are times, for reasons known to Him alone, that God does whatever He wants. He doesn't have to explain Himself to us, neither does He look favourably at our constant analysing of His actions and motivations.

Then the LORD answered Job out of the storm. He said: "Who is this that darkens my counsel with words without knowledge? Brace yourself like a man; I will question you, and you shall answer me. "Where were you when I laid the earth's foundation? Tell me, if you understand. Who marked off its dimensions? Surely you know! Who stretched a measuring line across it? On what

were its footings set, or who laid its cornerstone – while the morning stars sang together and all the angels shouted for joy?
(Job 38:1-7)

He is not our chum, our buddy, or our go-to man. He's not too happy being our last resort when everyone else lets us down or everything else fails. He is the great mystery and paradox, the majestic Person who has the affairs of the whole World in His hand ...

For since the creation of the world God's invisible qualities – his eternal power and divine nature – have been clearly seen, being understood from what has been made, so that men are without excuse.
(Romans 1:20)

... but also the loving and patient Father, willing and able to listen to and answer our prayers, however trivial.

Do not be anxious about anything, but in everything, by prayer and petition, with thanksgiving, present your requests to God.
(Philippians 4:6)

God is our Big Father and He loves us, indeed He is the model of the perfect father, Our Father in Heaven. And we need to learn to trust Him, totally, implicitly, even when things don't seem to make sense. Just as a toddler will stare resentfully at his father after the pain of the vaccination needle, not understanding the beneficial effects, so also do we need to suffer pain and confusion in life, often accompanied by a clenched fist raised to the sky, simply because we don't understand the full picture of our life's journey.

Satan may be the "god of this World", but God is in full control at all times. Understanding that may help us to understand this ...

Question: Why are not all healed?
Answer: God

Question: Why do some good Christians die prematurely?
Answer: God

Question: Why are there natural disasters?
Answer: God

Question: Why do evil men sometimes prosper?
Answer: God

Here you go, in each example we cut to the chase. We acknowledge that there are unique narratives behind every story of a lack of healing or early death and there is no simple formula to account for what may seem to be a failure of faith, or the effect of sin. Each story is far too important to those affected by the drama. Yet there is a sense that the full story is known to God alone, as it straddles this World and the World to come. God is the beginning and God is the end of everyone permitted to taste life, however brief, long, happy or unhappy that may be.

The four questions are perhaps the most persistent cries from the human heart, since the days of the Psalmists. They are birthed from hearts full of desperation, despair and confusion but, no malice or hurt is intended when I say that our perspective is not always *His perspective*. With that in mind, let us revisit those questions and imagine what God may answer:

Why are not all healed? *So that I can implement My plan for their lives and for those with whom they come into contact or influence.*

Why do good Christians die prematurely? *So that I can implement My plan for their lives and legacy and for those whom they influenced.*

Why are there natural disasters? *So that I can implement My plan for the lives of all involved.*

Why do evil men sometimes prosper? *I get them in the end! Read what I wrote in Psalm 73.*

Yes, this is simplistic and it doesn't consider and explore all circumstances behind each question. It may also have painted a very cold and distant picture of God, which is not the intention as it is God's love that holds everything together, despite what it may seem. There are many factors that come into play with all four scenarios, but this is only from *our* perspective. We bring up the question of sin and the fallen state of creation and the wiles of the devil and his minions and all have their part to play in *the Great Drama*, but it all boils down to one thing.

From God's perspective, it is all about Him. It always was and it always will be.

... I am God, and there is no other; I am God, and there is none like me. I make known the end from the beginning, from ancient times, what is still to come. I say: My purpose will stand, and I will do all that I please.
(Isaiah 46:9-10)

The LORD does whatever pleases him, in the heavens and on the earth, in the seas and all their depths.
(Psalm 135:6)

I don't like this God (you may well say).

Whatever you may think, this is the same God Who is more familiar as the God of love:

Whoever does not love does not know God, because God is love.
(1 John 4:8)

Let us consider this God of ours, this wonderful, loving, holy, supreme and sovereign God of ours.

Here He is, the Creator of everything in the Universe, from the amoeba to the supernova. He decides that, out of all Creation, only the human race is going to experience fellowship with Him. Not all are going to want to do so, but He wants to give all a chance, so He unfolds a plan. He allots every human being a time span on Earth, unique in length and circumstance, and, in ways known only to Him, gives everyone a chance to receive Him or reject Him. Those who receive Him are granted fellowship with Him forever, allowed to avoid the inescapable consequence of rejecting His love.

Yet to all who received him, to those who believed in his name, he gave the right to become children of God.
(John 1:12)

So when we weigh up our finite lifetimes of pain and struggle on Earth against an eternity of life with God, any real tragedies we experience here are a tiny blip in the complete story and may even have been allowed to happen simply to nudge us onto the right path.

The Hebraic understanding of God is one of reverence and respect. It is of acceptance of His majesty and greatness and seeks to please Him, for no other reason than He is the Creator of the Heavens and the Earth. The Greek mind is not completely satisfied by this and wants to know how God ticks. It seeks to know the unknowable, understand the un-understandable (that's a new word!). To the Greek mind, the intellect must be exercised, even if this exercise is futile. This is why there have been wars over doctrine. They haven't been wars about God Himself, but about competing understandings of the Father, the Son and the Holy Spirit.

The Israelites of the Old Testament fought their wars either as instructed by God or in defiance of Him. Victory depended on which of these options they took. If they acknowledged God and did what He asked, then He gave them victory in battle.

For the LORD your God is the one who goes with you to fight for you against your enemies to give you victory.
(Deuteronomy 20:4)

Christians of the medieval Church era and onwards fought their wars not over God Himself, but over interpretations of their beliefs in God. They were doctrine wars, not "holy" wars. This is not to diminish the importance of sound doctrine of course, but many times these disputes were over conflicting views, neither of which were sound doctrine!

Dear friends, although I was very eager to write to you about the salvation we share, I felt I had to write and urge you to contend for the faith that was once for all entrusted to the saints.
(Jude 1:3)

Christians, it is time for us to get real with our God, our Creator and our Father. Let's never forget, the Greek mindset puts *man* at the centre of things, the Hebraic mindset puts *God* there. So we need to put God firmly into the centre of our lives. I again ask, *how do we actually do this?* You may find these suggestions useful:

◊ Don't expect Him to rubber-stamp all of *your* plans and actions, even if they are from a sincere desire to exercise your gifts and are consistent with Biblical principles and seem to be in His will. God is the Great Ruler but He is also the great *Over*-ruler. We need to develop humility when our plans don't bear fruit and acceptance of God's correction. Sometimes through our zeal we can even obstruct God's plans, as in the story of the leper that Jesus healed.

A man with leprosy came to him and begged him on his knees, "If you are willing, you can make me clean." Filled with compassion, Jesus reached out his hand and touched the man. "I am willing," he said. "Be clean!" Immediately the leprosy left him and he was cured. Jesus sent him away at once with a strong warning: "See that you don't tell this to anyone. But go, show yourself to the priest and offer the sacrifices that Moses commanded for your cleansing, as a testimony to them."

Instead he went out and began to talk freely, spreading the news. As a result, Jesus could no longer enter a town openly but stayed outside in lonely places. Yet the people still came to him from everywhere.
(Mark 1:40-45)

The key word here is *instead*, showing the effects of the leper not doing what he was told but, instead, telling everyone about Jesus, which actually had negative effects in this instance.

◊ Avoid intellectual battles with atheists on trying to *prove* the existence of God. You are unlikely to convert them, however good your arguments are, as the real blocks to accepting God are spiritual and emotional, rather than intellectual, despite what they may say or think. By doing so you are using Greek tools, following in the footsteps of Thomas Aquinas and Anselm, influenced by the rationalism promoted by Aristotle. It's the heart that is the problem, not the mind. (Though there's my book, *The Truth is Out There*, written for atheists and their ilk, to point them towards the evidence of God's actions!)

The fool says in his heart, "There is no God."
(Psalm 53:1)

◊ Don't support any ministry that acts as if God is their servant rather than their Master. There used to be a TV ministry that went by the name of "What God can do for you". How man-centred is that? Just another consumer choice, to compete alongside spiritualism, socialism and veganism.

About ten years ago something called "The Prayer of Jabez" appeared. Oy Vey, what a triumph of marketing. How a short passage of Scripture can be expanded into a how-to book, describing new ways to manipulate God and sell nine million copies, takes my breath away. Just keep that fella away from Psalm 119!

The prosperity preachers need at least one mention. To promote Christianity as a financial investment with guaranteed returns is a most awful corruption and an affront to everything the Gospel stands for. God does not bless little green prosperity handkerchiefs or heal through bottles of holy water. God is not a special guest invited to special gatherings. *Yes, and he's come all the way from Heaven, to perform his miracles and healings ... let's put our hands together for ... (and please give generously).* This is not to say that God doesn't ever turn up at these meetings, as it's part of His gracious nature to work out His plans despite *our* plans. And He's never double-booked!

But there were also false prophets among the people, just as there will be false teachers among you. They will secretly introduce destructive heresies, even denying the sovereign Lord who bought them – bringing swift destruction on themselves. Many will follow their shameful ways and will bring the way of truth into disrepute. In their greed these teachers will exploit you with stories they have made up. Their condemnation has long been hanging over them, and their destruction has not been sleeping. (2 Peter 2:1-3)

◊ Think before you speak. If God devoted one of His ten commandments to a dire warning about misusing His name, then we must sit up and take notice.

"Oh my God!", "God help me" and their ilk can be heard in offices, homes and schools throughout the nations. God calls this blasphemy and there are consequences for such flippancies, so be warned. One place you'll never hear this word (or read it) is in a synagogue or in a religious Jewish home.

Yes, you may say, *it's because they use the Hebrew word for it, you're trying to trick me!* No, religious Jews have such a reverence for God that they can't even write or say His name. When a scribe was copying Scripture onto a new scroll and came across the name of God, he had to use a special quill to write this most holy of names.

In conversation these days, when referring to Him they use the word *HaShem*, which simply means "The Name". They take the Third Commandment seriously! When they need to write His name down they miss out the vowel and write either G–d or L–rd. It is a practical reverence and, to be honest, for some it is borderline superstitious, but the intention is sincere.

Many Christians use the Lord's name in vain without even realising it. Just exclaiming the name of God or Jesus, even if it is in code form or thinly disguised, is more of a casual disrespectfulness than a reverent invocation and one day you may have to stand in front of Him and explain yourself!

You shall not misuse the name of the LORD *your God, for the* LORD *will not hold anyone guiltless who misuses his name.*
(Exodus 20:7)

◊ Be thankful, in everything, not just at mealtimes, a practice that is not limited to Christians, but is practised by many faiths. Do we say grace when we snack between meals, or if we are eating alone with no-one to impress/satisfy or am I the only hypocrite here? The realisation that God is ever-present in our inner life as well as our comings and goings should provoke in us a sincere desire to thank Him for just about everything.

In Old Testament times, the thank offering was a spontaneous act, but it involved killing something, which may have taken a little of the spontaneity out of the act. We are under a better Covenant, sealed by the blood of Jesus, which ought to be in itself a reason for continuous praise and thanks. Nevertheless, I am endeavouring to be thankful in all things, acknowledging the One who makes it all possible, with a *thank you, Lord*, sometimes even out loud! We should strive towards spontaneity in this and not to allow it to become a ritual, otherwise it becomes an unacceptable sacrifice.

Sacrifice thank offerings to God, fulfil your vows to the Most High,
(Psalm 50:14)

This list could go on forever, but the intention is to get us thinking Hebraically, in the sense of understanding that God, not us, is at the centre of everything. In time He will prompt us to many new ways to adjust our thinking, as long as we are open to the possibility of change.

Of course, a lot of this is plain to see and these few pointers may already be resonating with you. Hebraic thinking is what this book is all about and many of you may already be *Hebraic* in your thinking. You don't have to be Jewish, or Messianic, or especially holy or have any other qualifications to do so. Hebraic thinking ought to be what being a Christian is all about and many of you may already have got it! If so, then rejoice in it, major reprogramming is not needed in your case, though it's good to work through things that you may not have ever considered.

Above all we need to realise that we're all in this together and God wants nothing more than Christian brothers and sisters to grow together in their understanding of Him. We also have a responsibility to bring as many others as possible into this journey, particularly those who have strayed off the path, usually through no fault of their own.

Give thanks to the LORD, call on his name; make known among the nations what he has done. Sing to him, sing praise to him; tell of all his wonderful acts. Glory in his holy name; let the hearts of those who seek the LORD rejoice. Look to the LORD and his strength; seek his face always. Remember the wonders he has done, his miracles, and the judgments he pronounced.
(Psalm 105:1-5)

Small is Dutiful

Here's a statement I never thought I would make: *there's something we can learn from our secular Government.* It's called *Big Society.* Of course, it's just a grand scheme and probably will never actually work in reality, but it makes some good points.

◊ Empowering individuals and communities – decentralising power from central government.

◊ Encouraging social responsibility – these small groups to act in their community.

◊ Creating an enabling and accountable state – flexibility in how the whole thing works.

What would happen if the Church in this country took heed of this? Big Church – though, contrariwise, *Small Church* would be a better name for it.

Of course we have already read how the Church of the original apostles *was* a Small Church. Those first Christians met in each other's houses for fellowship and mutual encouragement and instruction, which empowered them to reach out into their community, whether in the temple and synagogue or in the market squares and public meeting places. Government of these assemblies of "called out ones" was through an informal system of elders, selected from within their number, aided by those itinerant apostles, drawn from the close confidants of Jesus himself (with notable additions, such as Paul). So, if we had to define the *Small Church* of the first Christians, we would get the following:

◊ Empowering individual churches.

◊ Encouraging evangelism and social action for individual churches.

◊ Creating an environment for individual churches to operate without interference.

Of course many modern churches already operate under this principle, notably the house churches and the smaller independent evangelical churches, but they are far from being the norm. Today's Church as a whole, both as a product of historical processes and as a reflection of today's society, still likes to "think big".

That rag-tag group of around 120 ordinary folk on that awesome Day of Pentecost has morphed into a worldwide network of vast ecclesiastical corporations.

The Roman Catholic Church has over a billion members, 2795 branch offices (dioceses), over 400,000 managers (priests), controlled by a CEO (Pope) and a board of directors (Council of Cardinals). In 1994 it had an annual profit of $4 million, with $200 billion in cash deposits and several billion dollars worth of solid gold and other treasures in the Vatican vaults.

It takes just over £1 billion a year to run the Church of England, financing 13,000 parishes and 43 cathedrals. Around 15% of this comes from its financial assets, which amounted to £4.4 billion in 2008.

The Methodist Church finance division has a mission statement that offers practical solutions which combine Christian ethics and investment returns. This is not an attack on them, as I'm sure there are not many finance houses that have mission statements that offer Christian ethics as a foundational principle, but I wonder what John Wesley would think about a denomination growing from his efforts boasting £336 million of assets and that can offer a 42.8% return from its UK Equity Fund?

Like any corporation, these huge edifices seem mainly to exist to serve their own assets – welfare of staff, management of funds, investments and properties and maintenance of public relations to protect the brand name. So here are just three of the main denominations in the UK, all sitting on a lot of cash. How can we respond to this? With cynicism, anger or sorrow? Possibly all three. One question we should ask is whether this is all money well spent, in terms of the Gospel of Jesus Christ and what the Church is meant to be doing in the 21st Century.

The Church of England has seen a steady decline in Church attendance, running at around the million mark every week. The Catholic Church has also seen numbers drop, particularly in the ten years since 1996, but it has steadied itself since. The Methodists are in freefall with around a 10% drop every year in active churches.

So does that tell us that the Church in the UK is in terminal decline? It suits the secularists to believe so, who look just at the Catholics and Anglicans as barometers of the spiritual climate. Our media, too, when looking for Christian commentary or responses, tend to nab the nearest dog-collar, or, if particularly well connected, will grab some words from a bishop or even archbishop. It's sound-bytes they want, not commentary, so where better to go than to the media-trained apologists for liberal State Christianity?

But Christianity is *not* completely limp and dying in the UK, you just need to look a bit harder! There's actually a lot going on, lots of programmes, strategies, campaigns and initiatives. The Church really likes to do things big: The Call, Global Day of Prayer, March for Jesus (RIP), Pentecost Festival, Big Church Day Out, Spring Harvest, Alpha, all mobilising Christians in their tens of thousands, or worldwide in their hundreds of thousands. These days most Christian initiatives for worship, prayer and celebrating our faith are big corporate events, the bigger the better. A prominent media ministry, led by a very solid and charismatic teacher, has recently embarked on a programme to get one million people praying worldwide, and for this sheer force of numbers to prod God into revival action! Does it *really* work that way? A very large Church in the USA has so many folk coming to its services that it has to employ teams of volunteers as greeters, hosts, section hosts, traffic and transportation co-ordinators, ushers, translators, even medical alert response personnel (in case the preacher gets you worked up slightly too much!)

Through radio, TV and the Web, the whole World can watch major events, beamed out from packed stadiums and conference centres, but now multiplied in coverage through cable, wireless and the airwaves. Conferences, crusades and rallies for teens, women, men, Pentecostals and whatever. Big, big, BIG! Everything has to be global, world-reaching, mega-this and mega-that.

Christians in the USA are so desperate for revival that they create "happenings", such as the Todd Bentley *Lakeland* fiasco, the *Kansas student awakening* and the *Bay of the Holy Spirit revival* and ensure that they are propagated through satellite and social media, so that others can be "blessed" through the electronic transference of the anointing (find that one in your Bible!) Yet neither these, nor Toronto and Pensacola that preceded them, changed (or will change) the world one iota, unlike the true revivals of the past (and some in the present, in the developing World), such as the Methodists or the Moravians mentioned in an earlier chapter.

Apparently more than 2.5 million people had received Jesus Christ as personal saviour at a Billy Graham Crusade by 1993. It's a shame that there are no statistics on how many of those folk are still of the same mind now, but consensus opinion indicates just a small number. Perhaps the cynical, superficial, post-modern mind is no longer a good fit for such 'pre-packaged' mass evangelism, although of course the Holy Spirit can still work wonders with whatever raw material He has to work with!

Our current Western society delights itself with big happenings in stadia, from sports events, to pop and rock concerts. It's where our modern day 'icons' come to be idolised; that's why people come to such events. However, they may delude themselves or rationalise it as *just coming for the good vibes*. These places are designed for worship, perhaps that's why so many big Christian campaigns and outreaches tend to make use of football grounds. The big question is whether God prefers to be worshipped in such a way. Is the aroma of our worship more pleasing when facilitated by mega watts of electronic amplification?

There's a current initiative trying to raise £1 million to book Wembley stadium for a single event to get thousands of folk praying together. Bearing in mind they've done this before with no discernable effect nationally, is this a God-thing (Hebraic) or a man-thing (Greek), dressed up as if it were a God-thing? Do you honestly believe God would condone the use of money just to emulate the way the World does things?

It may seem logical that 80,000 folk worshipping together is 80,000 times more awesome for God than someone alone on her knees in her prayer closet, but is it Biblical?

Sure, in the Old Testament communal worship, based around the tabernacle or Temple, was the norm.

Then David said to the whole assembly, "Praise the LORD your God." So they all praised the LORD, the God of their fathers; they bowed low and fell prostrate before the LORD and the king.
(1 Chronicles 29:20)

But God has not provided us with geographical limitations for His worship any more. Until, that is, some time in the future …

Then I saw a new heaven and a new earth, for the first heaven and the first earth had passed away, and there was no longer any sea. I saw the Holy City, the new Jerusalem, coming down out of heaven from God, prepared as a bride beautifully dressed for her husband. … The nations will walk by its light, and the kings of the earth will bring their splendour into it. On no day will its gates ever be shut, for there will be no night there. The glory and honour of the nations will be brought into it. Nothing impure will ever enter it,

nor will anyone who does what is shameful or deceitful, but only those whose names are written in the Lamb's book of life.
(Revelation 21:1-2, 24-27)

Until then, we do the best that we can.

Now we see but a poor reflection as in a mirror; then we shall see face to face. Now I know in part; then I shall know fully, even as I am fully known.
(1 Corinthians 13:12)

Doesn't God prefer to deal with His people in their weaknesses and in their vulnerabilities? Isn't this the Biblical pattern?

But he said to me, "My grace is sufficient for you, for my power is made perfect in weakness." Therefore I will boast all the more gladly about my weaknesses, so that Christ's power may rest on me. That is why, for Christ's sake, I delight in weaknesses, in insults, in hardships, in persecutions, in difficulties. For when I am weak, then I am strong.
(2 Corinthians 12:9-10)

Didn't God choose Moses as a great inspirational leader although he was "slow of speech and tongue"? Wasn't Gideon the least significant member of the weakest clan of Israel, yet God chose him to defeat the Midianites? Wasn't Saul from the least clan of the least tribe, yet he became King of Israel? Similar story for David, the greatest King of all! Even Israel, His chosen nation for revealing Himself to the World, was "the fewest of all people".

God hasn't changed His ways. Surely it is more in God's revealed character to respond to Mrs O'Grady and her good friend Doris, meeting daily for prayer in their living room than with the Reverend Prophet Luke Atmee, broadcasting his religious declarations thrice daily from his gold encrusted pulpit in his million dollar cathedral of glass and steel.

God doesn't do numbers.

In Chapter 7 we looked at the three core features of the Hebraic mindset:

◊ Living Hebraically – God centred lives.

◊ Thinking Hebraically – thoughts driven by faith in God.

◊ Acting Hebraically – actions inspired by faith in God.

What do we want to do? Surely we want to *live* Hebraically, we want God in the centre of our lives, helping us to do things His way, not according to our schemes, strategies and programmes.

So now we apply the brakes. Let's wind down, slow down, allow our vision to diminish, to contract, to allow God to breathe, to transition from this thundering deity of the stadiums and the mega-Churches to the personal God who lives within us through the Holy Spirit and who assures us that, *when two or three gather* ...

Does not God work best as that still, small voice, away from the noise and the clamour, in the privacy of your own space, with fellow Christian sojourners, in your home or in small groups? This is the Hebraic way and I believe this is still the best way for the Church to move forwards. It may take longer, but then look at revivals from the past to see how swiftly and effectively whole nations were turned round just by small groups of people powerfully used by God, with no more than individual voices, carried from place to place by foot or horseback.

We go back further, to the Biblical Church of the first apostles. In the first section of this book I asked whether it is truly possible to return to a true Acts 2 Church, where:

They devoted themselves to the apostles' teaching and to the fellowship, to the breaking of bread and to prayer. Everyone was filled with awe, and many wonders and miraculous signs were done by the apostles. All the believers were together and had

everything in common. Selling their possessions and goods, they gave to anyone as he had need.
(Acts 2:43-45)

We have seen how these Christians met in homes, shared everything, exercised their gifts and had a very loose organisational structure. And that brings us nicely to that thorny subject of leadership. How did that all work out for them? Surely the words of Jesus echoed in the ears of those who had heard these words first hand:

Jesus called them together and said, "You know that the rulers of the Gentiles lord it over them, and their high officials exercise authority over them. Not so with you. Instead, whoever wants to become great among you must be your servant ... "
(Matthew 20:25-26)

How many of our Christian leaders are true servants? Some may say they are, some may even give the appearance they are at certain times, but how many really have a *heart of servanthood* ? The problem is that in society at large, leaders tend to float to the top through sheer force of personality and often with ruthlessness. That's how the *Gentiles* did it in Jesus' day. That's how our captains of industry, our directors of corporations, our CEOs and managing directors tend to get there. Certainly not through servanthood.

And the Lord's servant must not quarrel; instead, he must be kind to everyone, able to teach, not resentful. Those who oppose him he must gently instruct, in the hope that God will grant them repentance leading them to a knowledge of the truth ...
(2 Timothy 2:24-25)

The way of the Gospel is not the way of the World. Christian leadership is a quality best detected in a person by those who surround him or her, by those who have worshipped and studied with them, preferably in the context of a small group, the best environment for true relationships to develop. As a rule, the best Christian leaders are the last people to see the quality in themselves. But not all of them. Some of our Christian leaders, alas, have personality types more in common with Rupert Murdoch than Mother Theresa.

And this is how the Biblical Church of the first apostles selected their leaders.

So the Twelve gathered all the disciples together and said, "It would not be right for us to neglect the ministry of the word of God in order to wait on tables. Brothers, choose seven men from among you who are known to be full of the Spirit and wisdom. We will turn this responsibility over to them ..."
(Acts 6:2-3)

These were the first deacons, chosen from among the believers as men full of the Spirit and wisdom. Do we promote from within and how do we make our choices for church leadership? Perhaps you already do so, following sound Biblical instruction. But are all our church activities in line with how the Bible advises? Let's return to that very first description of the activities of that very first Church.

They devoted themselves to the apostles' teaching and to the fellowship, to the breaking of bread and to prayer. Everyone was filled with awe, and many wonders and miraculous signs were done by the apostles. All the believers were together and had everything in common. Selling their possessions and goods, they gave to anyone as he had need.
(Acts 2:43-45)

Let's delve deeper ...

They devoted themselves to the apostles' teaching ...

What teaching do we receive? Is it the apostles' teaching? How do we really know if we are receiving sound teaching? How do we judge it? Do we discuss it or examine the Scriptures, as did the Bereans, *"to see if what Paul said was true"* (Acts 17:11)?

Whether we receive this teaching interactively through Bible study or through the efforts of gifted, anointed preachers, we need to maintain a steady diet of good, solid Biblical meat and learn to discern any meat deemed, by the yardstick of Holy Scripture, as unfit for consumption.

This is so vital, so central to everything and will be discussed in the next section, when we explore how to *think* Hebraically.

... and to the fellowship, to the breaking of bread and to prayer.

Do we really get time to interact with each other, to discuss the things of God rather than the trivialities of life? What is our understanding of the 'breaking of bread'? Is this referring to Holy Communion, in which case, how did they partake of this memorial of Jesus' acts at the Last Supper? Every indication is that it was in the context of a fellowship meal, derived as it is from the Jewish Passover service, a noisy and evocative family occasion that, of course, survives to this day. How much of what we do is dry ritual rather than a spontaneous celebration of our glorious standing in God's Kingdom? How much prayer is there and is it spontaneous or just one element of an order of service?

Everyone was filled with awe and many wonders and miraculous signs were done by the apostles.

Does the supernatural ever break in? Does God ever show up in power? When was the last time you were filled with awe in church? A good friend was telling me that at one of their small group meetings a lady from within the congregation quietly prayed over each person in the room and had prophetic words for each of them.

Each word was relevant and encouraging, made more awesome by the fact that she did not know the folk well enough to be able to voice these words without there being a supernatural element. God evidently spoke through her and everyone was filled with awe. So it can still happen today!

All the believers were together and had everything in common. Selling their possessions and goods, they gave to anyone as he had need.

Are you a true, sharing collective or a group of private individuals who just meet up for a couple of hours every week? If one of you had a need would you share it with others? Would you respond sacrificially to another's needs? Would you sell your possessions and goods to meet these needs?

Or am I being unrealistic? Have we just moved on from that simpler World? Is it just not possible to "do Church" in the same way as those first believers? History is littered with many who have tried and failed, so why bother?

I think it's still worth giving it a go, after all, what is there to lose? And so much to gain. How marvellous would that be, worshipping God together with like-minded people in freedom and expectation. Imagine the following Scripture as a write-up of your church in the Christian press, after a visit from a "mystery worshipper".

They broke bread in their homes and ate together with glad and sincere hearts, praising God and enjoying the favour of all the people. And the Lord added to their number daily those who were being saved.
(Acts 2:46-47)

Let's think again as to what the word "Church" actually means. Earlier we discovered that the Greek word translated as "Church" actually means *called-out ones*. The word identifies us as people of God, though it has been used to refer to the building in which we meet. If we take these two thoughts together, it implies that the folk who meet *inside* these buildings are all called-out ones. That is untrue, as there are very few church buildings that can boast a congregation of 100% born again believers! We need to change our thinking away from what is man-made, to what is God-made.

But then we can take this even further. Again I ask, what is Church? Looking through the Scriptures it is true that in many cases the references are to the *Church at* ... Antioch, or Jerusalem, or Corinth etc., single churches or local groupings of churches.

News of this reached the ears of the church at Jerusalem, and they sent Barnabas to Antioch.
(Acts 11:22)

But in other places, what is being spoken of is the Church as a single entity, the complete Body of Christ, the worldwide collection of called-out ones.

But Saul began to destroy the church. Going from house to house, he dragged off men and women and put them in prison.
(Acts 8:3)

We can identify with the first, the local church, but, with over 38,000 denominations, it's very hard to see our current Church as a single entity. The best we can do is to speak regionally, as in the *English* Church, or refer to the larger groupings as the Catholics, Pentecostals, Presbyterians etc.

One more time I ask, what is Church ... for you? Is *Church* just people you meet with in a building, whether a church building, a leisure centre or a home, or is your vision wider than this? Does your church meet with other churches for missions or campaigns or prayer? Do you feel just as connected with these folk or are there barriers, of doctrine or personality or strangeness? When you meet other Christians, say at college or at work, in the context of group prayer or just fellowship, do you see this as Church? Is there a spiritual connection, something that crosses natural barriers, or do we retreat to what is familiar when we think about "doing Church"?

And what about accountability? The need for this was driven home to me through a recent tragedy, the suicide of an old friend through the stress of work. This has affected me deeply. This friend, a kind and easygoing family man, was just *not* the type of person who would resort to such a terrible solution to whatever was troubling him. Had he no-one on whom he could unload these troubles? We can only pray that his soul was reconciled to God before the final darkness. *There but for the grace of God we go* came to mind, not just as a trite slogan, but as a reality, an understanding that being accountable to each other is a gift, an outworking of God's grace in our lives.

See to it, brothers, that none of you has a sinful, unbelieving heart that turns away from the living God. But encourage one another daily, as long as it is called Today, so that none of you may be hardened by sin's deceitfulness.
(Hebrews 3:12-13)

We so need to look out for each other, particularly so in the Body of Christ, so that we can correct and encourage each other and help each other through problems that may even sneak up on us without our knowledge and harden our hearts. We tend to be individualists by nature and we may come out with a whole load of excuses for not binding ourselves with others: *I don't need to, I'm accountable to God alone. Nobody needs to know my business. I manage OK by myself.* All cop-outs.

Recently we spent a couple of days on Lindisfarne, Holy Island, off the North East coast of England and the cradle of Christianity in these lands. It's geographically unusual in that it is only accessible when the tide is out and there are great dollops of time every day when the island is isolated from the mainland, cut off by the sea. *No man is an island* said the Christian poet, John Donne in the 17th Century, yet how many of us live much of our lives in isolation, cut off from each other, if not from God.

The way of a fool seems right to him, but a wise man listens to advice.
(Proverbs 12:15)

As iron sharpens iron, so one man sharpens another.
(Proverbs 27:17)

Living Hebraically is all about relationships, with God and with fellow believers. To get this right we need to be in the right place, with the right people, with God at the centre.

Isn't it time we got serious? For many folk their church experience has become a habit, an obligation, even a chore. Perhaps it is because they haven't yet responded heart and soul and mind to God's free gift, in which case they are *not* the church, they are *not* the "called out ones". You and I are the Church. As a *church* we have an obligation to reach the World, but first we must learn to *live Hebraically*, we must get our relationships right with God and fellow believers.

Surely the best environment for nurturing these precious relationships is in a manageable group of folk who meet regularly, are accountable to each other, who can help to discover and nurture each other's gifts, and who can truly share in a safe, intimate environment. I don't think that is *ideally* realised in a mega-church, an internet church or in a church system that sees you just as a passive pew-sitter, though of course anything is possible when God acts in the lives of His people.

What then shall we say, brothers? When you come together, everyone has a hymn, or a word of instruction, a revelation, a tongue or an interpretation. All of these must be done for the strengthening of the church.
(1 Corinthians 14:26)

Wherever God has put us, let us strengthen one another, as best as we can, with the gifts that He has freely given us.

Family Matters

There's an unbroken line that connects you to Adam, the first human being. It's a parental line that twists and turns geographically and socially as it unfolds through history, one generation at a time. My own line drifted east through the steppes of Russia, and was then transplanted by rickety boat to the East End of London. Other stories are less or more dramatic, but we all have one. And one thing connects us, we are all birthed into a *family*, even if it is a family of one, a lone mother carving out a precarious life in a hostile world.

God chose it this way. It was His way of populating the Earth. It may not be the most clean, tidy and pain-free way (ask any mother). From our perspective, it may not be the most financially efficient way (ask any father), but it's the way that God chose. It goes right back to the Garden of Eden.

So God created man in his own image, in the image of God he created him; male and female he created them. God blessed them and said to them, "Be fruitful and increase in number; fill the earth and subdue it ..."
(Genesis 1:27-28)

Adam and Eve were fruitful, numbers were increased, setting the pattern for generations to come, until the whole earth was filled with people. They were the first married couple, bound together by *covenant*.

> *You ask, "Why?" It is because the LORD is acting as the witness between you and the wife of your youth, because you have broken faith with her, though she is your partner, the wife of your marriage covenant.*
> (Malachi 2:14)

Jesus confirmed the pattern.

> *"Haven't you read," he replied, "that at the beginning the Creator 'made them male and female,' and said, 'For this reason a man will leave his father and mother and be united to his wife, and the two will become one flesh'? So they are no longer two, but one. Therefore what God has joined together, let man not separate."*
> (Matthew 19:4-6)

So boy meets girl, they enter into covenant with each other, then have kids, who, in turn, meet someone else and keep the thing going. That's the mechanism that God put into place for mankind to fill the earth. Celibate priests aren't going to do the job and neither are alternative lifestyles, but that's a can of worms best left sealed for now.

The institution of family is God's building block for righteous living and we can trace this through the pages of the Bible.

Abraham, the father of our faith, had an extended family, including many that he had "acquired" in Haran, who had schlepped around with him in an ancient fleet of mobile homes. His son Isaac and grandson Jacob may have carved out their lives elsewhere geographically but they kept in touch. These extended families were called clans and, by the time we reach

Moses and the wilderness experience, there were hundreds of them, divided into the twelve tribes of Israel, named after the sons of Jacob.

And the focus of these clans was not in the great gatherings, but in the simple family home. In fact wasn't the Exodus itself, the great escape from Egypt, implemented on a family-by-family basis, with each household responsible for its own redemption, the first Passover?

On that same night I will pass through Egypt and strike down every firstborn – both men and animals – and I will bring judgment on all the gods of Egypt. I am the LORD. The blood will be a sign for you on the houses where you are; and when I see the blood, I will pass over you. No destructive plague will touch you when I strike Egypt.
(Exodus 12:12-13)

At the head of these clans and extended families was the father of each household. Joshua, the leader who followed Moses, was one such head. He made it clear to the others, who *really was* the head of these family households.

But if serving the LORD seems undesirable to you, then choose for yourselves this day whom you will serve, whether the gods your forefathers served beyond the River, or the gods of the Amorites, in whose land you are living. But as for me and my household, we will serve the LORD.
(Joshua 24:15)

The family motif runs right through the Hebrew Scriptures and in that great prophetic statement in Zechariah 12, when the house of David and inhabitants of Jerusalem will mourn for the one they have pierced, it will be the clans, the families, of the land that will mourn.

The first Church, as we have seen, met in homes, *family* homes.

The churches in the province of Asia send you greetings. Aquila and Priscilla greet you warmly in the LORD, and so does the church that meets at their house.
(1 Corinthians 16:19)

Day after day, in the temple courts and from house to house, they never stopped teaching and proclaiming the good news that Jesus is the Christ.
(Acts 5:42)

When this had dawned on him, he went to the house of Mary the mother of John, also called Mark, where many people had gathered and were praying.
(Acts 12:12)

After Paul and Silas came out of the prison, they went to Lydia's house where they met with the brothers and encouraged them. Then they left.
(Acts 16:40)

They rushed to Jason's house in search of Paul and Silas in order to bring them out to the crowd.
(Acts 17:5)

Greet also the church that meets at their house.
(Romans 16:5)

So did the second church and the third church etc., all the way to Constantine, when, as we read earlier, it all sadly changed. The Church was taken from the people and turned into a huge worldly corporation, with impressively constructed and ornately bejewelled branch offices, called churches and cathedrals, which were swiftly sanctioned as the only places where you could find God.

What was going on in folk's homes at that point then? For family homes in the "Christian" world, the situation could perhaps

be summarised by one word, *Ichabod*, "the glory has departed ..."
The practice of your Christian faith is what you did *outside* of your
home in the controlled environment that was the medieval church
building. Most families now lived in poverty, in small sparse
homes within small communities controlled by nobles, barons
and ... bishops.

The glory had departed! But not totally ...

While the "Christian" was living in poverty, ignorance and
subservience, kept in place by the promises of the "next world",
what of his Jewish neighbour?

The Jewish home was always intended as a holy place, a
sanctuary. The Jews had realised this when they were exiled to
Babylon about a millennium earlier. They no longer had access
to the focal point for their worship, the Jerusalem Temple. Did
this mean that God was no longer accessible? No, they may have
lamented by the rivers of Babylon, but they came to realise that
they could worship God where they were, in their homes and at the
synagogues, communal meeting places that were springing up in
this land of exile.

When the Jews were exiled yet again by the Romans in the
1st Century, the Temple was destroyed and this time the rabbis
formalised the new relationship, declaring that every Jewish home
should become a holy place, referring to it as a *miqdash me'at*, a
"small sanctuary". The home was to be a place for worshipping God,
a holy place. Tradition tells us that, when the Temple was destroyed,
the *shekinah*, God's Glory, didn't settle in the synagogues, where
you would have expected it to, but took up residence in every
Jewish home. God was truly identifying with the people where they
lived. Isn't this a profound yet wonderful thought?

*Therefore say: 'This is what the Sovereign LORD says: Although I
sent them far away among the nations and scattered them among
the countries, yet for a little while I have been a sanctuary for
them in the countries where they have gone.'*
(Ezekiel 11:16)

In the Greek Western mindset *one's home is a castle*, insulated from the outside world by a moat of separation, safe within its walls, protected from the *enemy without*. It has become a perfect expression of the individuality that has become the dominant theme for living in today's World. Is this how God really meant us to live? The dualism of Plato finds subtle and insidious expression in the lives of many Christians, separating their sacred and secular existences, living their lives in peace and isolation in homes, surrounded by Xboxes, plasma screens and all the materialistic trappings, while "doing Church" once or twice a week in "consecrated" buildings somewhere else.

The Hebraic, Biblical, mindset breaks down this division and sets aside each family home as a holy sanctuary, a mini temple. In Jewish tradition God was present in the place where they slept, ate and gathered together as families. A home is to be a "house of prayer" for the worship of God. It is to be a "house of study", for the learning of God's Word. It is also to be a "house of assembly", a place where people are welcomed. Added to that it is also to be a "house of eating and drinking", a "house of sleeping", a "house of making love" and so on. Try doing that lot in a "consecrated" church building and see how far that gets you!

Let's now pause and consider. In Old Testament times, as God gradually revealed Himself to His people, the accent switched from the big corporate manifestations – the revealing of the Law to millions of them at Mount Sinai or the massive throngs of people bringing their sacrifices to the Jerusalem Temple for the festivals – to the smaller, intimate occasions, in the synagogues and homes. In the New Testament, arguably the only big corporate manifestation in the life of the Church, was at its very birth.

When the day of Pentecost came, they were all together in one place. Suddenly a sound like the blowing of a violent wind came from heaven and filled the whole house where they were sitting. They saw what seemed to be tongues of fire that separated and came to rest on each of them. All of them were filled with the

*Holy Spirit and began to speak in other tongues as the Spirit
enabled them.*
(Acts 2:1-4)

Apart from the inevitable outdoor preaching engagements of the
apostles, all the building up of God's people and the development
of their relationship with God now took place within the confines
of the family home. That's how the Church started, a fact that I
have relentlessly and unashamedly reinforced! Yet this smallness
and this intimacy was soon lost as soon as Greek ideas took hold,
aided and abetted by the usual companion vices of greed, power
and avarice. This is a major point – we have been *sold a croc* and
we need to rediscover the path that has been lost.

So we have home worship and we have the context of family
as the norm. Let's run with this a bit longer as we return to the
typical home of a Jewish family living in exile and in constant
danger from their Christian neighbours. We have learned that the
home was considered a sanctuary, a holy place, a place where God
was happy to meet with His people, even if these were a people
with an incomplete grasp of His fullness, not being believers in the
incarnation and saving powers of Jesus the Messiah.

The home was the Temple (worship centre) and the dining table
was considered the altar (focus for fellowship). Even the everyday
act of eating is celebrated with spiritual connotations. Does that
mean that Jews worship food? Well, yes ... but that's just my
personal experience (in the same ways that other cultures may be
said to worship drink, gambling, sex etc.) and not relevant here. No,
Jews don't worship food, or drink but religious Jews consider eating
as a sacred act and the dinner table will also function as a place
where words of godly wisdom are exchanged in the conversations
that accompany the eating, where Hebrew prayers resound.

Continuing with the Temple imagery, the family would sing
songs of praise to God, as did the choirs in Solomon's temple. The
father, the head of the family, would function as priest, instructing
his family in the *Torah*, the teachings of God. In fact the Hebrew

word for parent, *horeh*, has the same root as *moreh* and *torah*. The latter two words mean "teacher" and "teaching", so a primary role of a Jewish parent is as a teacher. Traditionally the three roles of a Jewish father are to support his family, study the Bible (Torah) and see that his children study the Bible.

The rabbis tell us that *the world is poised on the breath of schoolchildren* and the education of Jewish children was always seen as an absolute priority. The Talmud (Mishnah Avot 5:21) tells us what sort of education these kids would have received, at the time of Jesus. It started at the age of five, when Bible training started, first from the Book of Leviticus, to understand the rituals and then from the Psalms, to understand the nature of God. At the age of ten, study began on the Oral Law and at the age of thirteen one was old enough to fulfil the laws and commandments. At fifteen they learned the works of the sages.

OK, so what's all this to do with 21st Century Christians living in a very different society, in terms of needs and expectations? It's all very well describing what we *should* be doing, but the fact remains that, for whatever reason, a household in the modern Western world is very different from a traditional medieval Jewish home. Let's not get all blurry eyed and Fiddler on the Roof and all that!

You may be a parent living with your spouse and 2.4 children. Or you may be divorced, re-married, single or *living unorthodoxly.* You may have a family full of step-children or adopted kids, it may not even be a biological one. Perhaps you are a collection of friends, or even a disparate group of folk somehow thrown together for any number of reasons. Your home may therefore contain a single generation, two generations, even three or more. We are a society of great variety in experience and circumstance.

A traditional family group worshipping God in the confines of a stable home environment may be the ideal situation, all things being equal. But all things are not always equal. So how can we *"do Church"* in the many strange lands in which we find ourselves?

On the one hand, this book is about moving forwards into the future, not judging the past and the present. On the other hand, there are the Biblical ground-rules. As Christians our primary relationship is with God, not each other and so our rules for living must flow from our relationship with Him, not from each other.

The Hebraic mindset is primarily concerned with our relationship with God, not with the rules and regulations that flow as a consequence (though I am not preaching lawlessness here). It's therefore primarily a matter of the *spirit* of the law, rather than the *letter* of the law.

You do not delight in sacrifice, or I would bring it; you do not take pleasure in burnt offerings. The sacrifices of God are a broken spirit; a broken and contrite heart, O God, you will not despise. (Psalm 51:16-17)

God is more pleased by our internal response to Him than by our external posturings. If we truly examine ourselves, our motivations and desires, particularly our life decisions, we must ask ourselves whether we are truly in line with God's revealed Word, however difficult that is going to be. And what is His revealed Word on matters of relationships and behaviour? It is the Bible, His revealed Word, ministered to our heart by the Holy Spirit and validated by our God-given consciences.

To understand what God's views are on these matters of relationships and behaviour we must strip away the multiple layers of human understanding, cultural nuances, media and peer pressure and simply ask ourselves whether what we are doing is in line with God's Word or whether we are using God's Word to validate our lifestyles by stretching and straining the text to accommodate our chosen conclusions.

So, what am I really saying? If we want to move on with God, whether or not it is to take onboard some of the ideas you have read about here, we must understand that there are two ways we can do this.

We can take the Greek approach, taking the man-centred position, using our human logic and understanding to justify ourselves and make ourselves comfortable in our chosen lifestyle. We do this by finding others who tread the same path and follow what makes them comfortable. Perhaps there are Facebook groups of like-minded people, with tame theologians who have found new ways of reading the Bible to blur the edges and justify *alternative* behaviour.

> *A discerning man keeps wisdom in view, but a fool's eyes wander to the ends of the earth.*
> (Proverbs 17:24)

We will always find folk who will use the Bible to say whatever they want it to say. That is the Greek view and it is most certainly *not* God's way. The Hebraic approach is God's way because it simply poses the question, *what does the God as revealed in the Bible think of this?* Not what *could* the Bible *seem* to say about this. The focus should not be on the Bible, but the *God* of the Bible, the *author* of the Bible. It's no good believing that you've found some loophole in God's Word to make everything alright. God is not mocked, you are just deluding yourself if you think that He's happy to see His precious Word manipulated by human reason driven by concerns of the flesh.

Or, to say it in a less wordy manner, if you are living in a relationship that is not the one prescribed below, then you are not going to be moving into God's blessings.

> *"Haven't you read," he (Jesus) replied, "that at the beginning the Creator 'made them male and female,' and said, 'For this reason a man will leave his father and mother and be united to his wife, and the two will become one flesh'? So they are no longer two, but one. Therefore what God has joined together, let man not separate."*
> (Matthew 19:4-6)

So, what am I saying? Let's first remind ourselves of our context, the Hebraic mindset, specifically living Hebraically. The key feature of this is to live God centred lives, which means that our lives must reflect Him. This means that our relationships must be as godly as our current situations permit.

Because a Christian marriage is a covenant and producing a family is a command of God (... *be fruitful and increase in number* ... Genesis 9:7), then blessings are already flowing. If such arrangements are at the centre of a church then it seems that blessings will be multiplied. Further blessings will flow in any church with God at the centre, but He won't bless any where sinful relationships are allowed to flourish. It's there, in His word, it's non-negotiable.

Flee from sexual immorality. All other sins a man commits are outside his body, but he who sins sexually sins against his own body. Do you not know that your body is a temple of the Holy Spirit, who is in you, whom you have received from God? You are not your own; you were bought at a price. Therefore honour God with your body.
(1 Corinthians 6:18-20)

And it's God's blessings that we must surely strive for where possible. If your household or your church is based around stable godly relationships, whether as a biological family or as a group of Christian brothers and sisters, then the channel for blessing is in place, I believe, for God to do His work.

Therefore if you have any encouragement from being united with Christ, if any comfort from his love, if any common sharing in the Spirit, if any tenderness and compassion, then make my joy complete by being like-minded, having the same love, being one in spirit and of one mind. Do nothing out of selfish ambition or vain conceit. Rather, in humility value others above yourselves, not looking to your own interests but each of you to the interests of the others.
(Philippians 2:1-4)

Intermission #1: Living Hebraically.

In building a body of believers, as in building a home, we need to get the foundations right, otherwise the whole thing crumbles into dust. The last three chapters had a single theme, that of relationships, our life's connections, surely the bedrock of our Hebraic expression of our Christian faith. And the bedrock of the bedrock is our relationship with our Maker, our Sustainer and our Hope, God Himself.

Biblically, and thus *Hebraically*, God is the centre of everything. This does not mean that we have no free-will. The debating floor is riddled with the debris of battles between Christian intellects, with precious Scripture as the bullets shot out of weapons of rationalism. Mighty men of God have spent careers fighting over weighty issues of doctrine, analysing the motives and actions of God Himself. I'm not a Calvinist. I'm not an Arminian. I'm a Christian who believes God's word implicitly and refuses to dissect Him and analyse Him and chop Him up into little chunks. The Hebraic mind accepts both God's sovereignty and man's free will and simply asks that each of us accepts responsibility not only for our own salvation but also for our conduct that flows out of the new creation.

Do not merely listen to the word, and so deceive yourselves. Do what it says. Anyone who listens to the word but does not do what it says is like a man who looks at his face in a mirror and, after looking at himself, goes away and immediately forgets what he looks like. But the man who looks intently into the perfect law that gives freedom, and continues to do this, not forgetting what he has heard, but doing it – he will be blessed in what he does. (James 1:22-25)

Then there is the manner of our connections to each other. Are we connected in the most effective way, to be the very best witnesses, to get the best teaching and instruction, to be able to give the very best of ourselves back to God? I believe that the most effective churches were the very first ones, meeting in small groups, unfettered by the lure of greed and ambition that hierarchies provided, once Greek philosophy had entered the fray. And if these small groups can be based around functioning family relationships then even better.

"For this reason a man will leave his father and mother and be united to his wife, and the two will become one flesh." This is a profound mystery – but I am talking about Christ and the church.
(Ephesians 5:31-32)

If the marriage covenant is a profound mystery then it must be very special indeed to God, particularly as it relates to His own relationship to the Church. Therefore any individual church that has a family relationship at its heart is surely going to be a real channel of blessing.

Living Hebraically is when we put high value on all of these relationships and really work hard to get them right.

Gimme, Gimme!

It's the end of the year and we celebrate with the usual traditions. Newspapers are printing reviews of the past 12 months, the Queen has finalised her New Year's honour list, the TV channels are awash with compilations, repeats and old films. Oh, and Christian ministries send out their seasonal emails and letters, begging us for some of our year-end money!

Isn't it strange that it should be so? Secular charities don't have these kinds of promises:

> *Look at the birds of the air; they do not sow or reap or store away in barns, and yet your heavenly Father feeds them. Are you not much more valuable than they?*
> (Matthew 6:26)

> *So I say to you: Ask and it will be given to you; seek and you will find; knock and the door will be opened to you.*
> (Luke 11:9)

Yet Christian ministries never seem to have enough money and are forced to follow the ways of the World – e-marketing, fund raising strategies, appeal campaigns – to procure sufficient funds to keep going. The implication is that, whereas all ministries feel able themselves to devise the plans and strategies that define their unique mission, when it comes to financing the vision, for some of them, it's down to the usual secular marketing techniques. Why should this be? Has it always been so?

Here's the usual reasoning. *Ideally, if all was functioning as it is meant to be in the Body of Christ, financial resources would be flowing through the connecting arteries, governed supernaturally by the promptings of God. But for this to work, all within the Body would need to be supernaturally tuned, in order to hear these promptings, let alone react to them. But most don't, so there are blockages, resulting in our need to replicate these promptings ourselves through letter, email, fundraising campaigns ...*

Sadly, there is a measure of truth in this. Yet we need to believe that God is able to work despite the shortcomings of His people. So if He wishes to bless a particular endeavour, then He's not short of a Plan B, C or D, if Plan A hits a brick wall! And, of course, if He wishes to cut off a few branches from the *parachurch olive tree*, one way of driving this home if all else fails is to cut off the nourishing sap!

When secular charities and businesses run out of money there are usually two reasons: it is either from lack of demand for their goods or services or through mismanagement. If Christian ministries run out of money, it may also be mismanagement (we usually call it bad stewardship) but we must accept that it may be God calling it a day on these specific activities. Perhaps the ministry has already fulfilled its commission and it's now just running on memories of past triumphs – though He never gives up on us as people, He simply redeploys us.

Anyway, why do we need so many ministries? Are they all divine commissions or, as I have been guilty of myself in the past, honest expressions of personal enthusiasm – *here I am God, use me, and here's how we're going to do it ...*

What ministries do we see in operation in the Book of Acts? Well, there are the individual churches, house churches dotted around Jerusalem, Samaria and the rest of the known World. All the financial needs of these ministries were nothing to do with infrastructure, but all about the needs of the people, whether in the congregation or elsewhere, with administrators assigned to organise the wealth redistribution, starting with the first seven deacons.

All the believers were together and had everything in common. Selling their possessions and goods, they gave to anyone as he had need.
(Acts 2:44-45)

There were no needy persons among them. For from time to time those who owned lands or houses sold them, brought the money from the sales and put it at the apostles' feet, and it was distributed to anyone as he had need.
(Acts 4:34-35)

So it seems that the financial needs of the early Church were met through the redistribution of wealth, so that no-one in the Body of Christ was needy. And that was it. No funds were used in the creation of hierarchies, with attendant salaries, accommodation and travelling expenses. No funds were used for any other purpose than the material needs of the Christian family, whether local, national or international.

Since then, as already noted, the Christian Church has become very much a collection of multinational corporations, national structures, as well as a variety of local expressions. If we were truly *One Body* then the financial needs of all surely could be met. The Catholics with their $200 billion and the Anglicans with their £4.4 billion and all the other denominations could all pool their cash and redistribute it just like those deacons in the early Church. Mmm …

But we are not really One Body as Paul envisaged it in Ephesians. We are multinational, national and local bodies, connected vertically but not horizontally, like a collection of individual puppets with a single puppet-master.

There is one body and one Spirit – just as you were called to one hope when you were called – one Lord, one faith, one baptism; one God and Father of all, who is over all and through all and in all. But to each one of us grace has been given as Christ apportioned it.
(Ephesians 4:4-7)

This speaks to me of a *single* body, the Body of Christ, not a collection of bodies. If we were truly a single body, think how effective we *could* be. There would be no competition between ministries over vision and resources, no wastage, no division, no conflict between believers. We would all individually be directly answerable to God, with a clear mandate of our position in the Body of Christ. The fact that this is not the case is mainly due to the Greek thinking that has inflicted the Church with structures and hierarchies and conflicting visions.

But again one must say, *we can do nothing about the past and the present; how do we move on to the future? Do we throw everything out and start again? Does God still bless us, despite the mistakes of the past? What, then, should our attitude be to God's provisions for us?*

Dare we move out of our comfort zones and trust that God meets all our needs as He seems to promise us in the Gospels?

Look at the birds of the air; they do not sow or reap or store away in barns, and yet your heavenly Father feeds them. Are you not much more valuable than they?
(Matthew 6:26)

In the last section we discussed how to live Hebraically, by getting our relationships right with God and with each other. With that sorted, the next consideration is how do we *think* Hebraically, how do we reflect God within us? Are our thoughts centred on Him? By concentrating on God's desire for us, rather than our needs, surely we must have sufficient faith to believe that our Heavenly Father will always look after us. So why aren't more of us *living by faith*, living from day to day without liquid assets or a set income?

Well, easier said than done, because our society conditions us to a view of work heavily influenced by Greek thinking. It's the way the World works – an employee enters a contract with an employer to give of his time, skills and talents in return for money, in the form of wages. It's a convenient arrangement, it makes sense and it works. But not in *every* case ...

Once you have become a new creation you enter a new kingdom, God's Kingdom. It's a wonderful place, full of blessings and promises, but a different place.

For the kingdom of God is not a matter of eating and drinking, but of righteousness, peace and joy in the Holy Spirit.
(Romans 14:17)

For the kingdom of God is not a matter of talk but of power.
(1 Corinthians 4:20)

Just as the Word of God, the Bible, is a document best viewed through Hebraic eyes (more of this in the next chapter), the operation of God's Kingdom is best understood *Hebraically*, too.

What this means is that we can't just flit between both Kingdoms and expect them to operate in the same way. And this very much includes the ways by which God provides for His people.

Whatever you do, work at it with all your heart, as working for the Lord, not for men, since you know that you will receive an inheritance from the Lord as a reward. It is the Lord Christ you are serving.
(Colossians 3: 23-24)

What this means in practical terms is that the Kingdom of God is not arranged logically, rationally, linearly ... these are all *Greek* principles, all very predictable and orderly but our God is far bigger than this. If God wants us to live the World's way, being rewarded with a day's wages for a day's work, that is fine. If God wants us to live in total reliance on Him, living by faith, then that's fine too. Also fine is any point in between these two positions. The key is to be *where God wants us to be*. And where He wants *you* to be is not necessarily where He wants *me* to be.

Living in God's Kingdom is an adventure and although God may plot safe routes through it for some people, to others He gives the grace *to ride the rapids*, to operate a little more dangerously. He will not impose Himself on us in any way that makes us uncomfortable. He will not take us beyond where we are able to go and, believe me, He knows us individually better than we know ourselves.

> *O Lord, you have searched me and you know me. You know when I sit and when I rise; you perceive my thoughts from afar. You discern my going out and my lying down; you are familiar with all my ways. Before a word is on my tongue you know it completely, O Lord.*
> (Psalm 139:1-4)

I know folk who *live by faith*, in fact one of my earliest introductions to Christians was to a husband and wife, John and Judy, who had just emigrated to Israel, living in Eilat, where I met them. I was on a "search for meaning" but they had found it. They took me in for a few days, in which time I was shown what living supernaturally was all about, as they never had two farthings to rub together, yet had a place to stay and the money to live by came on a day-by-day basis, through prayer and total faith in the expectation of God's provisions for them. Twenty five years later I met Judy again at a writer's course in London. She and her husband have been running a Christian hostel in Eilat and she was in the UK promoting her new book, *Walk the Land*.

My own experience as a freelancer working in the Christian media is that God has always provided for us when we needed Him to. That seems to be a sound Biblical principle, when we recall the Children of Israel in the wilderness, with the *manna* provided supernaturally daily for them to eat.

This is what the LORD has commanded: 'Each one is to gather as much as he needs. Take an omer for each person you have in your tent.' " The Israelites did as they were told; some gathered much, some little. And when they measured it by the omer, he who gathered much did not have too much, and he who gathered little did not have too little. Each one gathered as much as he needed. Then Moses said to them, "No one is to keep any of it until morning." However, some of them paid no attention to Moses; they kept part of it until morning, but it was full of maggots and began to smell. So Moses was angry with them. (Exodus 16:16-20)

Projecting this to the current day, although it may take a *whole lotta faith* on our part to live daily or even weekly in expectation of God meeting our exact needs, it does keep us focussed on Him on a continual basis, which is good for our souls, if not for our nerves! It helps us to see everything as a blessing, it makes us more thankful to God, the real provider of our needs, rather than the "middleman", your employer, who is simply the channel through whom God chose to work in your case.

Most of us Christians live our lives cut off from the true Source of all of our blessings. We live by supermarket opening hours, rather than by the success of this year's harvest or by the availability and well-being of livestock. Our daily needs come by monthly bank transfer not by daily prayer.

Rather than plead with individual Christians for the odd bit of cash, the ministries at the head of this chapter would surely be blessed more simply by asking God and *expecting* Him to act.

Ask and it will be given to you; seek and you will find; knock and the door will be opened to you. For everyone who asks receives; he who seeks finds; and to him who knocks, the door will be

opened. *"Which of you, if his son asks for bread, will give him a stone? Or if he asks for a fish, will give him a snake? If you, then, though you are evil, know how to give good gifts to your children, how much more will your Father in heaven give good gifts to those who ask him!*
(Matthew 7:7-11)

And if He doesn't, ask Him why not.

The 64 Million Dollar Question

Here's a question I posed at the start of my previous book, "How the Church Lost The Truth": *if the Bible is the Word of God, why is it apparently such a complex book to figure out with so many interpretations, understandings and misunderstandings?* I may have posed the question and hinted that the book would answer it, but, to be honest, it never really was totally answered. Perhaps it's an unanswerable question?

It's the 64 million dollar question for Christians today. Many have attempted to tackle it and many of these believe they have answered it, but have ended up creating more problems than solutions. Put yourself in the place of a new believer, someone who is embarking on an exciting new journey, having been "sold the idea" that all of life's problems and mysteries are dealt with in the pages of this one book, The Bible. So, spanking new Bible in hand, he turns up to his first Bible Study meeting and discovers that *Bible truth comes in many varieties!*

Has this always been so and, if not, what has changed to make it so? What was the function of Scripture in Jesus' day? Was it open even then to many different interpretations and understandings and, if so, what was the source of these different views? Were there different schools of thought among the Jews of his day as to how to interpret God's word?

These are perhaps the most relevant questions to answer because we know that, since Jesus' day, there have been innumerable schools of thought in the Christian world, largely thanks to the infiltration of the ideas of Plato and Aristotle. This is not for debate, as it is historically verifiable, and was fully covered in my previous book, *How the Church Lost the Truth*, where I demonstrated this history and also the origins of the various viewpoints regarding Creation, Israel, Hell, Salvation and End Times.

Just to flesh out these assertions a little, Plato introduced the idea of *dualism*, the separation of the physical and the spiritual, a pervasive concept that affected many aspects of the Christian life, including Bible interpretation. It gave rise to distorted views that the Old Testament (and the God of the Old Testament) was inferior to the New Testament, giving rise to Replacement Theology and also to the use of false allegory, in attributing grand but often random spiritual meanings to physical events in the Biblical text.

Aristotle championed the use of human reason to figure out the world. Alas, this also wormed its way into Bible interpretation, elevating human understanding to stand alongside divine revelation and thus blurring the edges between what is from the mind of man and what is from the Mind of God. This allowed folk to read their own ideas into Scripture and therefore coax the Bible to say whatever they wanted it to say!

Out of this Greek analytical thinking, the Bible was (and still is) prodded and poked, as if it were the shell of a rare bird's egg, ready to burst and spill out the reluctant secrets of its Author. New techniques for dissecting it are continually appearing, as if God really would provide us with His written word as source material for analysis, investigation and criticism rather than as *everything we need for life and godliness through our knowledge of him who called us by his own glory and goodness. (2 Peter 1:3)*

Here is a list of just some of these techniques, with the approximate date when they first appeared: *theological interpretation of Scripture* (2005), *biblical theology* (1787), *canonical criticism* (1983), *reception theory* (1970s), *intertextuality* (1990s) and *redemptive-movement hermeneutic* (1990s). And you *really* don't want me to describe and compare them, that's what Wikipedia on the web is for.

Some of you may call me an anti-intellectual, arrogant *so-and-so* for dismissing the work of so many great theological brains, but I am unapologetic about this because our focus must always be on God's work and not man's work. Suffice to say, if you want to mix up dry philosophic analysis with a lot of hot air, then by all means venture into these areas, but your time would be far better spent getting to know *the Author of the book* rather than by pulling His book to pieces just to prove your cleverness.

Where is the wise man? Where is the scholar? Where is the philosopher of this age? Has not God made foolish the wisdom of the world? For since in the wisdom of God the world through its wisdom did not know him, God was pleased through the foolishness of what was preached to save those who believe.
(1 Corinthians 1:20-21)

Atheists love it when we engage with them purely on an intellectual, philosophic level when discussing the Bible, because they know how easy it is to tie us up in knots, with such questions as, *can God create a rock so heavy He can't lift it* – if He can then he's not omnipotent and if He can't then He's also not omnipotent. Do we really need to exercise our brain cells in such a way? Can an atheist truly be won over to a *revealed faith* purely through the strength of your argument?

We hear of Christians living in the Third World who have such difficulty in finding access to a Bible in their own language, let alone actually owning one. And when they do get their hands on one, it is treated like a priceless gem and the words on the pages treasured for the spiritual jewels that they are. In the affluent West we can own Bibles in a myriad sizes, colours and versions, yet we are the ones living in poverty, *spiritual* poverty. We frame the unadulterated Scripture text with commentaries, daily reading plans (commentaries by any other name), books from our favourite Christian commentators and even more commentaries. We tend to shy away from the raw experience of quiet time with nothing more than a Bible in hand and a prayer for understanding on the lips. We do so, I believe, because of one of the cultural diseases of our modern age, *the cult of the expert*, the idea that we need to be told by others how to think about things. In the secular world, we all have our favourite reviewers for books, movies, music and it seems we also have them in the Christian world (me excepted, of course!)

Back to the 64 million dollar question. If God has created this book, the Bible, for us to live by, then which tools has He given us to gain the best from it? Is it a book that only the intellectuals and academics and theologians can understand and explain to the rest of us?

To answer this we need to enter deeper into the *Hebraic* mindset than we have yet dared to venture. To recap, we have summarised it so far into three areas:

◊ Living Hebraically – God centred lives.

◊ Thinking Hebraically – thoughts driven by faith in God.

◊ Acting Hebraically – actions inspired by faith in God.

To get the most out of reading the Bible we need to train our minds to *think Hebraically*. Not easy, as our western educational system is based on Greek rationalism, which is fine for understanding War and Peace, The Simpsons comic, or the Times editorial. But the Bible, God's Word, is a far different matter. It is a book authored by proxy, by God Himself. It's a supernatural book that speaks to us in some mysterious way that involves our minds and our spirits. There is the plain reading of it, of course, that we can all benefit from, believer and non-believer alike, with our *Greek* understanding. Then there are those times when God speaks to us individually, Spirit to spirit and Mind to mind. These are the times when we are interacting with Him *Hebraically*, we are open to Him because we are acting in perfect faith that He has a message for us.

But we can go still further because, although the Greek mind would read the Bible as any other book, the Hebraic mind would treat it as a living entity, an extension of God Himself and would seek to experience it not just through the mind, but also through the senses. In fact the Hebrew language has an awful lot going for it, despite being a set of strange symbols, read back to front. The best way to explore this is to see it in use. So we turn to the Bible, the beginning of the Bible, *right* at the beginning.

> *In the beginning God created the heavens and the earth.*
> (Genesis 1:1)

What did the great commentators from Church history have to say about this short verse?

Augustine, the commentator from the early Church revered by both Catholics and Protestants covers this in a long discussion as to why God decided to create the heavens and the Earth and concluded that it was *because He wanted to*, which is quite a neat answer really, but doesn't really add to our knowledge. In the Geneva Study Bible notes, the early Reformers (Luther, Calvin etc.) had very little to say about this other than to repeat the fact that God made everything out of nothing. Matthew Henry, the 18th Century commentator, adds little too, except to attack the *vain imaginations* of the philosophers. The great John Wesley is more forthcoming, making a reference to the Hebrew word used for God, *Elohim*, a plural word that seems to imply the Trinity.

So, apart from the snippet from John Wesley, they have little to say. Now let's turn to the Jewish commentators; what does the *Hebraic mind* have to say about this foundational verse? When the Hebraic mind has viewed this verse, the first thing we note is that it is the original Hebrew, *not* the English translation that is considered.

Bereshit	*bara*	*elohim et hashamayim*	*ve'et ha'aretz*
In the beginning	*created*	*God the heavens*	*the earth*

The Hebraic mind would look not just at the meaning of the words, but at the words themselves, and the letters of the words.

But first of all it would look at the plain simple meaning of the text, the *p'shat,* and would meditate on this. But then it would go further and deeper. It would ponder over the fact that this verse has 7 words and wonder why. Then it would ask why the first letter of the verse, in fact of the whole Bible, is a "B" and not an "A". Some have suggested that the "B" is referring to a big blessing (*bracha*) over Creation. They would also note that the first word, in Hebrew, *bereshit,* actually contains the second word, *bara*, reinforcing the truth that creation is truly at the beginning, and nothing came before it.

But, most wonderful of all, it would look at the words and wonder why the untranslatable word "et" was included dead centre in the verse, noticing that the two Hebrew letters in it are the *Aleph* and the *Tav*, the first and last letters of the alphabet. The Hebraic mind could perhaps take this further and think, *first and last, aleph and tav, where have I heard that before?*

Listen to me, O Jacob, Israel, whom I have called: I am he; I am the first and I am the last. My own hand laid the foundations of the earth, and my right hand spread out the heavens; when I summon them, they all stand up together.
(Isaiah 48:12-13)

God, *the first and the last,* the Creator Himself, including Himself dead centre in this first verse in the Bible. God, the Creator, identifying Himself in the creation of the heavens and the earth, the spiritual realms *and* the physical world, a truth that Plato and all who followed him, even in the Church, could never contemplate.

But a *Christian* Hebraic mind could take this further and now it gets very interesting indeed. This Hebrew word, "et", elsewhere in Scripture, when it is translated, takes the meaning of "sign".

Then the LORD said, "If they do not believe you or pay attention to the first miraculous sign, they may believe the second.
(Exodus 4:8)

Also, Hebrew being a pictorial language, every letter has a mundane association. The first letter of "et" is the *aleph*, pictorially depicting an ox, or a leader, a strong leader. The last letter, *tav*, pictorially is depicted by a cross, with the meaning of a "sign". So, we have food for thought, in that first verse in the Bible, a sign of the alpha and omega, depicted as a strong leader and a cross. It doesn't take much imagination …

OK, so I may have picked a particularly good example to demonstrate the incredible and fruitful world of Hebraic analysis, but this is just the tiniest tip of the largest iceberg; there's a whole universe of discovery out there.

You may ask what's the point of all this, why do we need to delve so deeply into Scripture that we find ourselves analysing not just words, but letters within the words? I believe it's because, once we know we can do it, we *should* give it a go. God has planted layers of meanings in His Word to draw us deeper into Him by faith. Of course it's not necessary for your salvation and not all are called to it, but why turn down a blessing?

It really is a deep shame that the Church has ignored its Hebraic roots for so long, because not only has it veered into error by consequence, it has cut off the root of its own blessing. We have lost our natural Hebraic minds and it's not something that can just be switched back in, but if God has planted the seed in you to try, then that is what you should do.

I had often wondered what Paul really meant by these words in Romans:

Again I ask: Did they stumble so as to fall beyond recovery? Not at all! Rather, because of their transgression, salvation has come to the Gentiles to make Israel envious. But if their transgression means riches for the world, and their loss means riches for the Gentiles, how much greater riches will their fullness bring! I am talking to you Gentiles. Inasmuch as I am the apostle to the Gentiles, I make much of my ministry in the hope that I may somehow arouse my own people to envy and save some of them.

For if their rejection is the reconciliation of the world, what will their acceptance be but life from the dead?
(Romans 11:11-15)

What did he mean by *riches for the world* and *life from the dead*? Could he have been looking ahead to a time when orthodox Jews, perhaps rabbis, with such deep knowledge of the Hebrew Scriptures in their raw form, finally have the veil removed from their eyes and meet Jesus, their Messiah? Think what they could offer the wider Church in terms of their Hebraic understanding? Some already have, such as Alfred Edersheim and Arnold Fruchtenbaum, but they are surely just the first fruits. But, until then, how do we move forwards?

How can we start to view Scriptures Hebraically? It's not going to happen overnight but a good start is to start reading up on the subject, though there are currently precious few accessible books on the subject. What we can do, though, is to develop an understanding of how *not* to understand the Bible. This was dealt with more fully in my previous book, *How the Church Lost the Truth*, but here are a few pointers.

◊ In the first instance take the plain simple meaning of the Scripture you are reading, the *p'shat*.

◊ Put yourself in the role of someone who would have heard the words in the original setting and how they would have understood the words in context.

◊ When you hear or read of an interpretation of a passage that doesn't ring true, or seems to re-inforce aspects of materialism, greed, individualism or popular psychology then you have probably encountered *eisegesis*, trying to find Bible verses (usually out of context) that seem to back up your ideas, rather than using the Bible as the initiator of the ideas.

Armed with this, let's have a new look at a famous passage:

For I received from the Lord what I also passed on to you: The Lord Jesus, on the night he was betrayed, took bread, and when he had given thanks, he broke it and said, "This is my body, which is for you; do this in remembrance of me."
(1 Corinthians 11:23-24)

Yes, very familiar, the beginning of the Lord's Supper liturgy in many churches. Yet, in context, it is a response to a certain situation. Let's read the preceding three verses:

When you come together, it is not the Lord's Supper you eat, for as you eat, each of you goes ahead without waiting for anybody else. One remains hungry, another gets drunk. Don't you have homes to eat and drink in? Or do you despise the church of God and humiliate those who have nothing? What shall I say to you? Shall I praise you for this? Certainly not!
(1 Corinthians 11:20-22)

Paul is having a strop, but it's not *that* I want to focus on, but the occasion itself. What's all this about eating and drinking? It's the *context* of the Lord's Supper in the early Church. It was not a dry ritual carried out on your behalf by a registered member of the clergy; it was something everybody did together, as part of a meal. Yet, thanks to the Greek Church Fathers, it had *become* a dry ritual, stripped from its rich context, which is why we only hear the later verses and not the build up verses, otherwise we'd all be making an almighty mess in the pews!

Here's another one:

What then shall we say, brothers? When you come together, everyone has a hymn, or a word of instruction, a revelation, a tongue or an interpretation. All of these must be done for the strengthening of the church.
(1 Corinthians 14:26)

I will rewrite this, to reflect the current situation in many churches.

What then shall we say, brothers? When you come together, no-one, apart from the clergy, has a hymn, or a word of instruction, a revelation, a tongue or an interpretation. All of these must be done (if there's time) for the strengthening of the church.

If the first Church did these things (the 1 Corinthians 14:26 list, not my revision), then why don't we? Are we selective in our Bible reading or have we just been conditioned to believe that a lot of the Bible is just not for the Church today?

The Bible is the most precious thing you could ever read. Treat it so, but never worship it, that honour is reserved solely for the *Author* of the Bible. Sadly, many Christians, with their constant analysis and arguing over the words of God, have in fact been worshipping the Bible of God more than the God of the Bible. They wallow in their own cleverness in their debates with other Christians and will fall out with each other over the smallest issues. Some would even quote Amos in their defence:

Do two walk together unless they have agreed to do so?
(Amos 3:3)

We all have our champions, our favourite Bible teachers who defend our doctrinal positions with skill and eloquence. They are our surrogates, our gladiators of the debating chamber. But sometimes such things can divide.

Keep reminding them of these things. Warn them before God against quarrelling about words; it is of no value, and only ruins those who listen. Do your best to present yourself to God as one approved, a workman who does not need to be ashamed and who correctly handles the word of truth.
(2 Timothy 2:14-15)

Perhaps we should develop the confidence to fight our own battles, read the texts for ourselves and develop opinions based on group study. The rabbis have always considered study of God's Word as the highest form of worship, so let us always bear that in mind as we delve into His Word.

Here's an idea. In my first book, How the Church Lost The Way, I mentioned a type of Jewish group study, called a *Beit Midrash* (House of Learning). It's like a home group format, but noisier and a tad unstructured. A traditional home group would follow the Greek model of having the pastor, minister, elder or teacher leading the meeting, perhaps linking material with the Sunday sermon, or following a thematic series.

A *Beit Midrash* doesn't need to be led by someone who has prepared well, or has all the answers. It needs a facilitator, someone to move things along, but the whole point of it is for everyone to learn together. If your minister wants to join in, then he's on the same level as everyone else and should not be allowed to dominate. The point of the Beit Midrash is the acknowledgement that sometimes we don't have all the answers, but it will be fun to find them out together. Proceedings are disorderly, a very Jewish idea, with interruptions, silences, jokes and tangential thinking all the norm. The one thing you won't need to do is put your hand up to speak, though you may have to deal sensitively with the situation of everyone speaking at once. The best way to try this form of group study is just suck it and see.

So, *thinking Hebraically*, that's what we need to strive for if we want to go deeper into God's Word.

"Come now, let us reason together," says the LORD ...
(Isaiah 1:18)

Sounds like a good invitation to me.

Yeshua ben Yosef

Which Jesus do you follow? Do you have an image of him in your mind when you pray or sing a worship song? Is it a Jesus from your childhood memories, perhaps the gentle brown-haired Jesus at the Da Vinci table? Is it a mystical Jesus, perhaps with a glowing heart and halo? Is it a baby Jesus, a richly adorned ecclesiastical Jesus, or perhaps the forlorn battered body on the cross? Or is it a Jesus restyled to fit in with your own culture? A white Jesus, a black or brown Jesus, an oriental Jesus? Why am I asking, does this really matter?

In one way it doesn't matter, after all doesn't the Second Commandment prohibit the use of images, or specifically idols that can be revered or worshipped?

You shall not make for yourself an idol in the form of anything
in heaven above or on the earth beneath or in the waters below.
You shall not bow down to them or worship them;
(Exodus 20:4-5)

But we have imaginations and sometimes it helps us to fix our mind on something visual when contemplating the Divine. It's when we take it one step further that we can hit problems.

Yassar Arafat, the PLO leader and ex-President of the Palestinian Territories, once said, "Jesus was the first Palestinian Shahid

(Martyr)". What he has done here is to wrench Jesus away from his true historical setting and place him into a false one, also attributing a false role to him. This is subtle propaganda for political purposes, but it sows seeds into minds.

In the Jewish Talmud, there's another twist on Jesus. In one account he is known as

Yeshu ben Pandera, Yeshu son of Pandera. Pandera was meant to be the name of Mary's lover, a carnal dig at the Virgin Birth. A curious embellishment is the insistence that Mary was a women's hairdresser, though this is likely to be a mistranslation, caused by a literary variation of "Chinese whispers". Pandera, sometimes called Stada as a nickname, was thought to be a Roman soldier. This whole scenario of course was a complete fabrication, a reaction to the bad things that were being done to Jews at that time in the name of Jesus.

Then there was the Jesus of the Nazi lunatic, Hitler. This Jesus was a blonde-haired Nordic type, of Aryan ancestry, without a drop of Jewish blood in his bloodline. What a surprise!

You've met the counterfeits, now meet the *true* Jesus in his true historical setting ...

Picture the scene. It's two thousand years ago, in a small village called Nazareth, in the Galilee region of what is now the Land of Israel. You see a little boy playing in the backyard among the wood piles and shavings. His father, *Yosef,* is in the workshop next to the yard and his mother, *Miriam,* is busy cooking. His name is *Yeshua ben Yosef.* You know him better as Jesus, son of Joseph.

It is time for lunch and his mother calls him. If Miriam had called him by the name 'Jesus', two things would have happened. Firstly, he would have carried on playing, not recognising the name and secondly, the neighbours would have been astonished at Miriam's bad attempt at Greek, a feat which was about as likely as your average cockney walking up to a pub landlord and asking for a pint of beer in his best classical Latin. If she'd added the epithet 'Christ', the situation would have been even more dramatic, because not only would he have continued to ignore her and the neighbours been astonished at her Greek, but she would also have been stoned to death for assigning a forbidden and blasphemous title to her son. That is because 'Christ', is the English translation of 'Christos', the Greek translation for the Hebrew word 'Mashiach', which means *Messiah*, or 'anointed one'. And no Jew would dare to make a claim to that title. Well, not until this particular boy became a man and embarked on his life's mission.

Yeshua (Jesus) was a nice Jewish boy, of whom any mother would be proud. He was born in Bethlehem, as the Christmas cards show us, in very humble surroundings. After birth he had been circumcised and consecrated at the Temple and, by all accounts, had the typical childhood of one from a poor family in a Galilean village. And how do we know they were poor? *"No room at the inn"* was certainly a clue but the clincher was the *"pair of doves or two young pigeons"* that they sacrificed to the Lord after the birth. This was the *pidyon ha-Ben*, the redemption of a boy. It's an acknowledgement that every first-born boy belongs to God and all parents must "buy him back" by making a sacrifice. This rule dated right back to the time of Moses, when the first-born boys of the Israelites were spared from the Angel of Death on Passover night. Joseph and Mary were too poor to offer a lamb sacrifice and so were permitted to offer up the birds as a cheaper alternative.

They were poor but must have been devout Jews. Not all families made the annual pilgrimage to Jerusalem, but Luke 2:41 tells us:

Every year his parents went to Jerusalem for the Feast of the Passover.

For poor people this was exceptional and tells us that God indeed made the correct choice in parents for Yeshua. Another clue is in the song, The Magnificat, sung by Miriam (Mary) when she visited her relative Elizabeth. This song alludes to no less than thirteen Hebrew scriptures, telling us that, even at a relatively young age, the mother of Yeshua was fully conversant with the Judaism of her day.

But what of Yeshua and his education? The Mishnah, a 3rd Century collection of the oral "Traditions of the Elders" tell us that Jewish boys of the day would study the Torah (The first five books of the Bible) at the age of five, the oral "Traditions" at the age of ten and be trained in *halachot*, rabbinic legal decisions at the ripe old age of fifteen! Sunday School was never harder! It was made harder still when one realises that reading material was scarce and a poor family like theirs would have, at best, just one or two Biblical scrolls, just a small part of the total breadth of Scripture. So much was committed to memory.

It was serious business being a 1st Century Jewish schoolkid! So what was Yeshua doing in those silent early years? He was hard at study, memorising Scripture and rabbinical commentary, in common with most other Jewish youths of his day. By the time he had left his adolescent years he would have memorised most of the written Torah. From then on his mother, Miriam, watched proudly as he '*grew in wisdom and stature, and in favour with God and men.*'

The boy became a man as Yeshua arrived by the banks of the River Jordan, where his relative, John the Baptist (Yochanan the Immerser) was 'preparing the way'. Baptise me, declared Yeshua. You've got to be kidding! responded John. Do I look like I'm kidding? Let it be so! The act of baptism, was, in the words of Alfred Edersheim, "the last act of his private life". This was some beginning to this unique and awesome ministry. Heaven opens and the Spirit of God descends like a dove and a voice from heaven proclaims, "This is my Son, whom I love; with him I am well pleased", a combination of Psalm 2:7 and Isaiah 42:1. The common interpretation of the symbolism here is of an expression of the Trinity; God the father commending God the Son in the presence of God the Holy Spirit, who takes the form of a dove.

Yeshua began his ministry. His deeds may have been mighty, but in appearance he was just like any other Jewish itinerant teacher. Far from the blue-eyed, chisel-jawed Hollywood Swede, or the dreamy ginger-haired Renaissance Italian, he was an olive-skinned, dark-haired 1st Century Jew. The Samaritan woman certainly thought so.

The Samaritan woman said to him, "You are a Jew and I am a Samaritan woman."
(John 4:9)

He certainly dressed as a religious Jew. A clue is in this passage:

Just then a woman who had been subject to bleeding for twelve years came up behind him and touched the edge of his cloak. She said to herself, "If I only touch his cloak, I will be healed."
(Matthew 9:20-21)

It's not an obvious clue, because the translation does the original event no favour at all. The clue becomes clearer when we look at the same passage in the Jewish New Testament translation.

A woman who had had a hemorrhage for twelve years approached him from behind and touched the tzitzit on his robe...

Spot the strange word? Tzitzit. Some translations refer to it as a "hem", which is only marginally more accurate than "edge". A better word is "fringe" or "tassel", a word that appears in Numbers 15:37-39.

The Lord said to Moses, "Speak to the Israelites and say to them: 'Throughout the generations to come you are to make tassels on the corners of your garments, with a blue cord on each tassel. You will have these tassels to look at and so you will remember all the commands of the Lord, that you may obey them and not prostitute yourselves by going after the lusts of your own hearts and eyes."

And that is what Jesus was wearing. A robe, like the garments worn by today's Bedouins, with tassels, or tzitzits, on each corner. It marked him out not just as a Jew, but one who followed the Torah and lived by it, as directed by that passage in Numbers.

He taught in synagogues and the Jewish Temple, without a Gentile in sight. Much of his teaching was in a thoroughly Jewish context. He visited Jerusalem for the Pilgrim Feasts of Pesach (Passover), Shavuot (Pentecost) and Succot (Tabernacles), as well as Chanukah (Dedication of the Temple) and made great use of their symbolism in his teachings, particularly when speaking of his mission on Earth. He went to great pains in affirming the great themes of the Old Testament, the only Holy Scriptures available to the Jews of his day.

Jesus answered, "My teaching is not my own. It comes from him who sent me. If anyone chooses to do God's will, he will find out whether my teaching comes from God or whether I speak on my own."
(John 7:16-17)

Yeshua (Jesus) the Jew, the spokesperson for God Almighty, the *man*. I emphasise the latter, because the Church has at times struggled with the idea of the humanity of Yeshua, the idea that God could walk this earth as a fully flesh-and-blood human being. Yes, it's that Greek philosophy of Plato rearing its ugly head again.

The problem is that the Greek thinking of the time could not get a handle on the concept of "the Word becoming flesh", as stated at the start of John's Gospel. For them everything physical, such as the human body, was basically evil, and the creation of an inferior god, whereas anything spiritual was basically good and the creation of a better god. Out of this craziness came an idea known as *Docetism*, taken from the Greek word for "to seem".

For followers of this heresy, Jesus only *appeared* to have a physical body, only appeared to eat and drink and talk and sleep and excrete bodily wastes. And if you have trouble considering the latter, then perhaps you, too, are a closet Docetist. That may seem a facetious comment, but it just shows you how ingrained these

Greek ideas are in the current Christian psyche. The Hebraic and Biblical view of our human existence is a holistic one, a seamless unity of mind, body and spirit. All are good and beneficial to our well-being. There's nothing crude and un-godlike about our bodily functions.

"Blessed be the LORD God, King of the Universe, who has created humans with wisdom, with openings and hollow parts, revealed before Your holy throne, that if any part of the body was to malfunction, it would be impossible for us to exist and stand before You even for a short time. You cure all flesh and perform wonders!"

Yes, this is the Jewish prayer for going to the toilet. All in life is a gift from God. Going to the toilet regularly is a blessing (to some more than others), no more or less than eating or receiving an answered prayer. All should be thanked for and all are present in the Jewish liturgy.

But the Greek Docetists weren't interested in the Jewish liturgy, they had rejected that long before, replacing it with the pagan ideas from Greek philosophy. For them *Yeshua* was no more human than Spiderman or Dan Dare. For them, God could never take physical form, because matter and flesh were evil, so he could only *seem* to have a body, he could only *seem* to be crucified, could only *seem* to be resurrected.

Utter rubbish. Try telling that to Simon Peter who ate fish with him or the woman who poured oil over him. Try telling that to the hundreds of Jews who met him in his lifetime. Try telling that to Mary who gave birth to him; tell her that her contractions were just an illusion!

Joking aside, this episode just goes to show how the truth can be the first victim when you are enslaved to an alien philosophy.

So, what have we learned? The greatest resource that God has given us was His son, Jesus. What is vital for understanding is to know *which* Jesus we are following, the Jesus of history, who walked the earth in ancient Israel as a Jew, with all the negative connotations that it entails.

Why is this important? It is important because it is true. It's not opinion or propaganda, it's a subject often glossed over because of the historic *Gentilisation* (is there such a word?) of the Church and the corresponding redrawing of Jesus the man. Conjure up an image of an orthodox Jew in a synagogue, covered with the *tallit*, the fringed garment, his head covered and his body criss-crossed with the leather straps and boxes of the *tefillin*. This was Jesus in the synagogue. Not an image that the renaissance artists would have contemplated.

Not only must we strive to understand the Bible of Jesus, but it's also important at all times to consider the authentic Jesus of the Bible.

Intermission #2: Thinking Hebraically.

We have seen how the foundations of the Body of Christ are the relationships therein and, if we don't get them right and our relationship with God the Father, how the whole thing crumbles into dust. There's another way we can scupper it and that is by starving it of sustenance, so our Heavenly Father has made sure that this doesn't happen. God has not only given us the structure, but also a mechanism to ensure it runs correctly. He provides us with practical resources to look after our body and spiritual resources to feed our soul.

In theory, we Christians should ask for nothing, doesn't our Heavenly Father meet all our needs? True Hebraic thinking ought to encourage us all to live in perfect faith for His promises.

Ask and it will be given to you; seek and you will find; knock and the door will be opened to you. For everyone who asks receives; he who seeks finds; and to him who knocks, the door will be opened. Which of you, if his son asks for bread, will give him a stone? Or if he asks for a fish, will give him a snake? If you,

then, though you are evil, know how to give good gifts to your
children, how much more will your Father in heaven give good
gifts to those who ask him!
(Matthew 7:7-11)

But the Lord has made us all different, with different situations,
needs and paths to tread. Some of us have been truly called out
and given the grace to live in total reliance on Him. This must be
such a blessing, as it implies a severance from the empty promises
that the world feeds us through the media, and a life transplanted
into the realm of true Kingdom living, a throwback to those vital,
exciting days of the first Church that I spoke of at the beginning
of this book. For the rest of us, I believe the more we lay our
lives bare to God and trust in Him, the more He will give back
to us and bless us. The *true* prosperity Gospel is the prosperity
of God's grace in our life, providing for our daily need as and
when we need it, as with the manna in the desert for the Children
of Israel.

The spiritual resources that God provides for us are totally
sufficient for our needs. He has given us His son, Jesus Christ,
without whom our lives would be without direction or hope. The
more we understand him in his true *Hebraic* context, the more we
can get from his teachings and the more blessed we will be. Surely
it can't get better than that!

And we can say the same for the written and living word of God,
the Bible. What many Christians don't understand is that, thanks to
the Greek hijacking of our minds we rarely get a chance to dig deep
into the true riches of His word just beneath the surface. Although
there are quick fixes, gems that we can share from the fertile minds
of those commentators who have trained their minds *Hebraically*,
a real deeper understanding can only come through diligent study.
And that is totally up to you, what are you waiting for?

Thinking Hebraically is when we learn to adjust our thinking
in terms of God's provisions for us and not to be distracted by
anything else.

A Good Reflection?

First, a reminder …

> *Do not merely listen to the word, and so deceive yourselves. Do what it says. Anyone who listens to the word but does not do what it says is like a man who looks at his face in a mirror and, after looking at himself, goes away and immediately forgets what he looks like. But the man who looks intently into the perfect law that gives freedom, and continues to do this, not forgetting what he has heard, but doing it – he will be blessed in what he does.*
> (James 1:22-25)

It's bad enough that we forget what we look like, but what do others really see when they look at us? Do we have a Sunday face, a smiley, earnest expression of benevolence that we switch on between journeys to and from our church? Do we even have a special social face that folk see when they meet us, very different from our normal expression when we're safe between the four walls of our homes? I have been told that I have a telephone voice, a *poshed-up* voice that I only use when answering the phone, but very different from the everyday drone. Of course, I fervently deny this! But then again …

Which is the *real* you? Are you reflecting on the outside what you're really going through on the inside, or are you equipped with a full set of masks as if life is just one big masquerade ball? Do we always feel smiley and benevolent on the inside?

Let's back-track a little. We have seen the importance of living Hebraically, in good relationship with God and man, and thinking Hebraically, with our thoughts governed by our faith in God. Now we must consider what is going to flow out of this arrangement, how we are meant to *act Hebraically*.

Do we have God centred lives? If this were so, then it ought to make a difference. So what are the boxes most likely to be ticked in a survey of "*How can you spot a Christian in your neighbourhood*"? Judgemental ... *tick*. Self-absorbed ... *tick*. Arrogant ... *tick*. These seem to be the badges of dishonour displayed by your average Christian living in the affluent West (though, of course, not always).

There's a common saying that the only Bible some folk will read is you. It's your actions, your good conduct, that is going to attract them or repel them. So we've got to make sure our conduct is ... good. Simple!

If we don't do this then the possibility for damage is immense, not just for individuals but also for the Church. Let's face it, in the UK the Church is seen as a joke, any respect for the timeless truths of Christianity undermined by the antics of our current batch of leaders. Here are some recent headlines in the secular press:

Church encourages worshippers into debt so they can donate more.

He's ignorant, crude and un-Christian. But don't expect the spineless Church to banish Bishop Pete.

'Bonking Bishop' loses dismissal claims over affairs.

Faith healer quits after 'unhealthy relationship' with female co-worker.

Notice that these headlines were from the *secular* press, not the Christian press. These stories – with fresh additions more-or-less daily – are read largely by non-Christians and serve to bolster the negative stereotypes of a crumbling monolith of diminishing influence, over-absorbed by in-fighting and only waking from its slumber to make the odd unwelcome political or social declaration, rather than Biblical proclamations or prophetic warnings.

Accountability faces outwards as well as inwards. Although all Christians have responsibility for each other, there's a broader picture painted. Our ultimate accountability is to God Himself – He who neither slumbers nor sleeps – and if He has put us in positions of responsibility within the Church, to the extent that we can feasibly have a national voice, then why do so few speak out with conviction, certainty and power? How many are bearing good fruit for the Lord?

Every tree that does not bear good fruit is cut down and thrown into the fire. Thus, by their fruit you will recognize them. Not everyone who says to me, 'Lord, Lord,' will enter the kingdom of heaven, but only he who does the will of my Father who is in heaven.
(Matthew 7:19-21)

Jesus says this about us:

You are the light of the world. A city on a hill cannot be hidden. Neither do people light a lamp and put it under a bowl. Instead they put it on its stand, and it gives light to everyone in the house. In the same way, let your light shine before men, that they may see your good deeds and praise your Father in heaven.
(Matthew 5:14-16)

Are we truly radiant people, do folk marvel at our good deeds and feel attracted to our God as a consequence? In some cases, yes, but mostly ... no!

The Hebraic way is social not individualistic. It can be summed up by one of the sayings of the Jewish sages, *little is gained for the progress of the world if one person achieves perfection and holiness.* Also, *do not segregate yourself from the community.* It stresses community all the time.

There's something else that we can learn from these Jewish sages and that is the true meaning of *joy.* The disciples certainly demonstrated it:

> *And the disciples were filled with joy and with the Holy Spirit.*
> (Acts 13:52)

No language has more words for joy than Hebrew. The sages declared that *joy is called by ten names.* Nearly every book in the Old Testament reminds us to rejoice in the Lord, especially the Psalms.

> *God has ascended amid shouts of joy, the LORD amid the sounding of trumpets. Sing praises to God, sing praises; sing praises to our King, sing praises.*
> (Psalm 47:5-6)

We Christians, who have far more reasons to know deep joy than anyone, should take note of such things.

At least folk should be able to see how different we are by the way we treat fellow Christians. After all, didn't Jesus say:

> *A new command I give you: Love one another. As I have loved you, so you must love one another. By this all men will know that you are my disciples, if you love one another.*
> (John 13:34-35)

How often do we hear people say, *look at those Christians, they may not have much time for us but see how they love each other?* I'm not saying that we don't have love for each other, but it's just that we are *not known* for this fact. It ought to be our mark, our badge and it may have been so in the early Church, but not so much now.

Of course there are exceptions. I can think of many of them, thank goodness, but I have also met many Christians who fit society's bleak stereotypes. We are told to be radiant and loving towards each other, but this is not how society perceives us.

I have an enormous admiration for our current Queen Elizabeth, arguably the only authentic Christian voice currently taken seriously in our country. On opening the 2010 Church of England General Synod, she said *"What matters is holding firmly to the need to communicate the Gospel with joy and conviction in our society."* It's a shame that the media would not report on that snippet but would rather report on other matters that concerned the Anglicans at this particular gathering.

So what did concern them? The big issues were homosexuality among the clergy and women bishops and how the Church of England can keep promoters and dissenters happy without causing a major split. And you wonder why we Christians are lampooned, ridiculed and cast into the dustbin of history as an irrelevance. If the only message the World receives from the "Church" concerns its internal battles and very public falls from grace, how could they come to any other conclusion?

We are therefore Christ's ambassadors, as though God were making his appeal through us. We implore you on Christ's behalf: Be reconciled to God.
(2 Corinthians 5:20)

Ambassadors? An ambassador's job is to represent his country and people in the most favourable light possible. Who are the true ambassadors for God in our World? I suggest that it is not the usual suspects, the salaried 'men of the cloth', with their grand titles and their ecclesiastical pensions to look forward to. Men in frocks and dog collars don't do it for me, I'm afraid. No, God's ambassadors are those who take seriously their accountability to God to be a true, living and real witness in a World that has absolutely no idea how much it needs it. Real people, Christians like you and me, who have every chance of making a positive impact on the World.

Some have already broken through. Witness these stories.

Margaret Mizen had lost her 16 year old son just two days earlier to a moment of unprovoked madness by a young thug at a bakery. Yet here she was, on the UK media. *"I just want to say to the parents of this other boy, I want to say I feel so, so sorry for them. I don't feel anger, I feel sorry for the parents. We've got such lovely memories of Jimmy and they will have such sorrow about their son. I feel for them, I really do."* Margaret and her husband have spoken openly how their faith has helped them through this tragedy and their simple dignity has demonstrated this so clearly to the nation in subsequent years. They have since set up the *Jimmy Mizen Foundation* (www.jimmymizen.org) to help young people to live responsible lives.

She was the scourge of the "permissive society" of the 1960s and 1970s, but Mary Whitehouse was just an ordinary art teacher from Shropshire. Targeting the BBC, she campaigned relentlessly and seemingly single-handed to 'clean up TV', imploring it to *"encourage and sustain faith in God and bring Him back to the hearts of our family and national life"*. So her Christian faith was upfront and the clear inspiration for her efforts. Out of these efforts came the *National Viewers' and Listeners' Association*, now known as Mediawatch – UK (www.mediawatchuk.org.uk), though it seems, like many erstwhile Christian charities, to have wrenched itself free from its Christian roots.

It was at the height of the Irish troubles and one of the worst atrocities was the bombing at the Remembrance Day service in Enniskillen. Just a few hours afterwards, Gordon Wilson, the father of one of the 10 killed that day, publicly forgave the bombers on the BBC and asked that no-one would seek revenge for his daughter's death. A historian later remarked, *"No words in more than twenty five years of violence in Northern Ireland had such an emotional impact"*. Until his death in 1995 Gordon worked tirelessly and effectively for peace in that troubled land. His legacy is the *Spirit of Enniskillen Trust* (www.soetrust.co.uk), *working with young people for a shared future.*

Rachel Scott was the first student gunned down by the teenage killers in the school shooting in April 1999, later known as the Columbine tragedy. Rachel was a committed Christian and it was this that singled her out for what was later called a martyrdom. Her funeral was the most watched event on the CNN TV channel up to that point and her life was the inspiration behind an initiative, *Rachel's Challenge* (www.rachelschallenge.org), to *promote a positive culture change in schools and businesses.*

Yes, these are exceptional stories, but they all feature ordinary Christians who have sprinkled a touch of the grace of God into the World. They have not made declarations from the pulpit or the TV studio, but have demonstrated by their *actions*, their faith and good conduct that there really is something special about those folk who have the Holy Spirit living in their hearts.

But the sad news is that these exceptional stories may also be the exceptions. When the Barna Group in 2008 were looking at American divorce rates they noticed that: *when evangelicals and non-evangelical born again Christians are combined into an aggregate class of born again adults, their divorce figure is statistically identical to that of non-born again adults: 32% versus 33%, respectively.*

If there was one area where Christians could have demonstrated that living under guidance from the Holy Spirit actually made an observable difference to one's life, it's in the area of marriage. If Christian marriage, the anchor and the source for such blessing for solid family life, is held so sacred by a people *who have the operating manual on the subject,* how come it fails just as frequently as non-Christian marriage? It makes no sense and, in fact, makes a terrible mockery of what the Christian life is meant to be all about.

Recently, the Office for National Statistics in the UK noticed that just one in three churchgoers "actively practises" their faith compared with more than two-thirds of Muslims, Hindus, Sikhs and Buddhists. Christians are also less likely to say that their beliefs influence their everyday life, although they do affect the school to which they send their children. It's not a pretty picture, is it?

Is there really anything different about us Christians ... really?

The media thrives on bad news, negativity and the darker side of the human experience, so you would expect it to ignore the countless Christians who are behaving as they should, because *this ain't news*. What is news for them is when the pastor runs off with the bishop's wife, the choirboy or the church silver, or when some blinkered cleric makes a hugely insensitive remark about something or other. The media feeds on any story that reinforces the negative stereotypes, thus serving to cement these caricatures in people's minds. There must be a way to break free from this cycle.

Yes there is a way, but it needs us *individually* to break free. It's individualism that got us into the mess to start with, the secular lie that has so infiltrated the Church. It promotes the very humanistic Greek idea that puts us at the centre of everything. The Church has forgotten that very Hebraic idea that it is *God*, not man, at the centre of everything. To remind you:

Do not conform any longer to the pattern of this world, but be transformed by the renewing of your mind. Then you will be able to test and approve what God's will is – his good, pleasing and perfect will.
(Romans 12:2)

As Christians, we still, by and large, live for ourselves. This makes us no different from non-Christians in the way we act and this is why there are as many Christian divorces as non-Christian divorces.

Yet God, in His word, expects us to try a little harder. Here are a few clues to this:

For those God foreknew he also predestined to be conformed to the likeness of his Son, that he might be the firstborn among many brothers.
(Romans 8:29)

And we, who with unveiled faces all reflect the Lord's glory, are being transformed into his likeness with ever-increasing glory, which comes from the Lord, who is the Spirit.
(2 Corinthians 3:18)

Just pause and consider this. God expects us to be remodelled into Jesus' likeness – not his physical Jewish features but rather his character and his nature. It's never going to be a complete transformation in this life as we have our sin natures forever dragging us back, but we need to allow the Holy Spirit to start cleaning us up and nudging us onwards. It's not something that is going to happen by magic, automatically. It's a joint effort between you and the Holy Spirit.

You are going to have to give some things up. Before I was a believer, I was an avid fan of horror fiction but since then I actually have felt faint and physically sick simply through picking up a Stephen King novel. God's promptings are there for a purpose.

You are going to have to change some attitudes and lifestyle choices. These can take time, depending on how deeply rooted some sin areas are in your life. You'll be surprised what God can do if you let Him, but you must be open to His ways and, just as with the dentist, a little pain may precede release and freedom. But, believe me, it will be worth it in the long run.

When people see you in the street, at the supermarket, at work, at ... do they see Jesus? Do they at least see a work-in-progress? Do they see anything that they don't see in themselves, that may prompt them to ask the sort of questions that we are desperate to answer? We want them to say, *hey we want some of what you've got*, not because of our devastatingly clever arguments but through the evidence of a changed life that they see in us.

So I tell you this, and insist on it in the Lord, that you must no longer live as the Gentiles do, in the futility of their thinking. They are darkened in their understanding and separated from the life of God because of the ignorance that is in them due to the hardening of their hearts. Having lost all sensitivity, they have given themselves over to sensuality so as to indulge in every kind of impurity, with a continual lust for more. You, however, did not come to know Christ that way. Surely you heard of him and were taught in him in accordance with the truth that is in Jesus. You were taught, with regard to your former way of life, to put off your old self, which is being corrupted by its deceitful desires; to be made new in the attitude of your minds; and to put on the new self, created to be like God in true righteousness and holiness. (Ephesians 4:17-24)

Let's face it, we've heard plenty of sermons on this, are quite familiar with the Bible verses and perhaps have read books on the subject, but Christian doctrine is of absolutely no use to us unless it travels from head to heart, from theory to practice, from knowledge to real application. It's an old cliché, but for many people the only Bible they read is *you*. We are being watched, usually by those wanting us to slip up, so why not surprise them and confound the stereotypes by demonstrating *the new self, created to be like God in true righteousness and holiness.*

The first Christians took these things seriously. Read the following account aloud and marvel as you realise just how seriously these Christians in Thessalonica took their faith. Paul was certainly impressed.

We always thank God for all of you, mentioning you in our prayers. We continually remember before our God and Father your work produced by faith, your labour prompted by love, and your endurance inspired by hope in our Lord Jesus Christ. For we know, brothers loved by God, that he has chosen you, because our gospel came to you not simply with words, but also with power, with the Holy Spirit and with deep conviction. You know how we lived among you for your sake. You became imitators of us and of the Lord; in spite of severe suffering, you welcomed the message with the joy given by the Holy Spirit. And so you became a model to all the believers in Macedonia and Achaia. The Lord's message rang out from you not only in Macedonia and Achaia – your faith in God has become known everywhere. Therefore we do not need to say anything about it, for they themselves report what kind of reception you gave us. They tell how you turned to God from idols to serve the living and true God, and to wait for his Son from heaven, whom he raised from the dead—Jesus, who rescues us from the coming wrath.

(1 Thessalonians 1:2-10)

But this was to change. As Greek thinking entered the Church, Christian doctrine became something to be argued over rather than something that dictates conduct and behaviour. Folk took the great Bible truths and indulged in fruitless discussion over them, producing great libraries of teaching and commentary, pure distractions from the pure, simple and direct commands of Holy Scripture. Out of this came the Catholic tradition that elevated these libraries to positions of Church authority, to be followed even if they directly contradicted the Bible passages that had once provided the inspiration for their authors.

Doctrine became all-important, necessarily so because of the rise of heresies, themselves a product of the infiltration of the ideas of Plato into Christianity. So suddenly the Church became a battleground fought by different shades of Greek thinking, with Plato arming both sides of the conflict. The biggest casualty of all these shenanigans was Biblical truth and application, thankfully preserved, as ever, by God's faithful remnant, working both at the edges and outside of mainstream Christian society.

Major Churches split over matters of doctrine, usually birthing a new denomination that itself, would invariably fracture into competing factions. Christians fought Christians with the force of their rhetoric and the force of arms. Priscillian, Bishop of Avila, and his followers were beheaded by Church authorities in AD 385 for living and teaching a life in accordance with Scripture, rather than accepting the corruptions of State Christianity. They were said to be the first Christians actually executed by the Church. Should conflicts over doctrine lead to beheadings – where does it say this in the New Testament?

If we consider ourselves "free range" Christians, with freedom to roam, study and worship, then the medieval Christian was most definitely *factory farmed*. Herded into imposing churches and cathedrals, their Christian life was defined by externalities, necessary actions called *sacraments*, rather than by any internal conviction or life in the Spirit. The common man had no access to the Bible or the great truths of salvation by faith in Jesus Christ. It's fair to say that very few were loved into the Kingdom in those days, the laity were too busy with the physical needs of surviving from day to day and the clergy were too busy basking in their debating skills and general disdain for the laity. Those outside the "church", such as Jews and Waldenses, were either mercilessly persecuted or evangelised at the point of the sword.

A new command I give you: Love one another. As I have loved you, so you must love one another. By this all men will know that you are my disciples, if you love one another.
(John 13:34-35)

Love was very much a missing ingredient in those brutal times, the Gospel had become fodder for debate and argument, not a blueprint for living godly lives.

Skipping many generations since then, though we are currently living in calmer times, we have unconsciously inherited this Greek attitude of debate over conduct. In many ways this is the source of the Christian stereotypes in the secular world. We must make no excuses for being judgemental, because we stand for uncomfortable universal truths, but quite often – putting it in modern vernacular – our attitude sucks. We often come across as self-righteous, miserable, boring, cold, humourless and arrogant because we are so certain of the rightness of our cause and the force of our arguments that we believe that this alone is going to convince others.

We are familiar with this:

But in your hearts set apart Christ as Lord. Always be prepared to give an answer to everyone who asks you to give the reason for the hope that you have ...
(1 Peter 3:15a)

But what about the rest of the verse?

... But do this with gentleness and respect, keeping a clear conscience, so that those who speak maliciously against your good behaviour in Christ may be ashamed of their slander.
(1 Peter 3:15b-16)

But the last word on this has to be with the apostle John.

This is the message we have heard from him and declare to you: God is light; in him there is no darkness at all. If we claim to have fellowship with him yet walk in the darkness, we lie and do not live by the truth. But if we walk in the light, as he is in the light, we have fellowship with one another, and the blood of Jesus, his Son, purifies us from all sin.
(1 John 1:5-7)

Walking in the light, what a concept! It's translating your internal convictions into external actions. It's all about doing stuff, not just believing it. It's about showing love to others, not just debating about it. It's about giving of yourself to others, not just being able to recite the relevant Bible verses. It's at the very core of a Hebraic attitude. If we do this, then we can really have true fellowship with each other, no hidden sins or agendas and, if sin does creep in, as it so often does, the assurance that the blood of Jesus deals with this on our behalf.

The Jews have an interesting word, *halacha.* It means "walking" or "the way to go", in the sense of rules to live by. Jewish halacha comprises the teachings of the Torah, interpreted by the rabbis through the oral teachings of the Talmud. It is a complete set of rules for living, covering all aspects of life and is in a state of continuous development, adapting itself to the ever-changing World.

We can take this and develop a *Messianic halacha,* rules that Jesus has given us to live by, so that we can be *walking in the light.* Our goal, of course, is to become like Jesus:

> *And we, who with unveiled faces all reflect the Lord's glory, are being transformed into his likeness with ever-increasing glory, which comes from the Lord, who is the Spirit.*
> (2 Corinthians 3:18)

To help us on the way, though, we too need a set of rules for living. Unlike the rabbis, although they base their halacha on the Hebrew Scriptures, they are as interpreted by the rabbis. We must base our *Messianic* halacha primarily on the New Testament, with the Old Testament also providing general instructions and principles.

If we walk in the light, keep the full counsel of God and *act Hebraically,* allowing our faith to dictate our actions and attitudes then perhaps unbelievers can really see Jesus reflected in us and want to know more about what makes us tick.

Let's pray that we may all show a good reflection.

CHAPTER 15

One New Man

One New Man. At the heart of this is an issue that divides, yet ironically it's a Biblical concept that is meant to do the complete opposite, bring folk together. It's a Jewish thing, which means you either know a lot about it or absolutely nothing. Either way, I believe it important enough to devote a chapter to it because it involves a spiritual malady that has deprived the Church of so much blessing that, unless it is addressed, will increasingly diminish the Church.

As I have already stressed, *Hebraic* does not mean *Jewish*. It is simply a convenient title for the mindset of Jesus, the first Christians and the characters who inhabited centre stage of the Old Testament. The fact is that they were Jewish, but that doesn't mean that every Jew since then has operated within a Hebraic mindset, though history has shown us that the Judaism that developed since the fall of Jerusalem in AD70 has had more Hebraic elements than Greek ones, in terms of reverence for God, the centrality of faith and the importance of good conduct.

But that *Jewish* thing! It's a contentious issue, fraught with danger and positively bursting with agendas galore. To be honest, if the front and back cover had indicated that this book had *Jewish* themes, however subtle, most of you would not be reading it. I can say that with total certainty, through personal experience as a writer who has written at least six books on such themes and has enjoyed critical acclaim but negligible sales.

Why should this be? Is the Church antisemitic?

I am tempted into bitter irony, with the reply, *is the Pope Catholic?* This is a double irony really as the "first Pope", Peter (Simon) was as Jewish as Woody Allen and as Catholic as ... Woody Allen! But I won't sink into self-pity but instead speak out of *real concern for the Western Church* by declaring that, *I'm afraid it is ... mostly.*

Here is an observation made in my earlier book, *"The People of Many Names".*

> *It is worth making a brief mention of the Melanie Philips article in The Spectator. On February 16, 2002 she wrote an article entitled 'Christians who hate the Jews'. She was reporting on a meeting of Jews and prominent Christians brought together to discuss the churches' increasing hostility towards Israel. She wrote 'The real reason for the growing antipathy [to Israel], according to the Christians at that meeting, was the ancient hatred of Jews rooted deep in Christian theology and now on widespread display once again . . . The Jews at the meeting were incredulous and aghast. Surely the Christians were exaggerating. Surely the Churches' dislike of Israel was rooted instead in the settlements, the occupied territories and Prime Minister Ariel Sharon. But the Christians were adamant. The hostility to Israel within the Church is rooted in a **dislike of the Jews**' (my emphasis).*
>
> *The Christians at that meeting affirming this view were the editor of the main Church of England newspaper, the Archbishop of Wales (now the Archbishop of Canterbury), the Middle East representative of the Archbishop of Canterbury and the head of a Christian institute and relief organisation, who remarked 'What disturbs me at the moment is the very deeply rooted anti-Semitism latent in Britain and the West. I simply hadn't realised how deep*

*within the English psyche is this fear of the power and
influence of the Jews.'*

To understand the reasons for this antipathy to the Jews would take
a book in itself (the aforementioned 'The People of Many Names')
but the crux of it is in the realisation by Derek Prince. In his teaching
letter (No. 7) on *The Root of Anti-Semitism*, he says this:

> *"While I was preaching in our local church in Jerusalem,
> quite unexpectedly I heard myself say, "Anti-Semitism can
> be summed up in one word – MESSIAH!!" At that moment
> I understood that from its beginning Anti-Semitism had one
> source – Satan – who was motivated by the knowledge that
> the One who was to be his conqueror, the Messiah, would
> come through a people that would be specially prepared
> by God."*

He goes on to explain that the Jews, the people in question, were
targets of Satan through their whole history, either through being
enticed into idolatry (early history) or through complete destruction
(later history). The reason for this hatred is that he knows that his
days are numbered, a countdown culminating at the return of Jesus
the Messiah.

**The fact that the established "Church" was (and still
is) the predominant tool used by Satan in this nefarious
scheme cannot be swept under the carpet.**

This issue will need to be addressed, not in the sense of "repenting"
for the sins of others in the past, but in a real sense of self-
examination. This may be a painful experience for some.

Antisemitism is very real, even in these *enlightened* times. The
Jerusalem Post reported that the number of antisemitic incidents in
the UK in 2009 was an all-time high, with 924 recorded. There has
always been a link to events happening in Israel and the troubles in

Gaza that year spilled over to the UK and other countries, provoking
hate crimes against Jewish populations.

This is big stuff and you may be hearing this for the first time.
Let's make a couple of points absolutely clear.

◊ The facts of historical "Christian antisemitism" are a matter of
proven record.

◊ The reasons for "Christian antisemitism" are in the spiritual realm
(ask any prayer intercessor) and have never been satisfactorily
explained in any other way.

Having established these provocative ideas, now for *One New Man*.
What is it?

*Therefore, remember that formerly you who are Gentiles by
birth and called "uncircumcised" by those who call themselves
"the circumcision" (that done in the body by the hands of
men) – remember that at that time you were separate from
Christ, excluded from citizenship in Israel and foreigners to the
covenants of the promise, without hope and without God in the
world. But now in Christ Jesus you who once were far away have
been brought near through the blood of Christ. For he himself
is our peace, who has made the two one and has destroyed the
barrier, the dividing wall of hostility, by abolishing in his flesh
the law with its commandments and regulations. His purpose
was to create in himself one new man out of the two, thus making
peace, and in this one body to reconcile both of them to God
through the cross, by which he put to death their hostility. He
came and preached peace to you who were far away and peace
to those who were near. For through him we both have access
to the Father by one Spirit. Consequently, you are no longer
foreigners and aliens, but fellow citizens with God's people and
members of God's household, built on the foundation of the
apostles and prophets, with Christ Jesus himself as the chief
cornerstone. In him the whole building is joined together and*

rises to become a holy temple in the Lord. And in him you too are being built together to become a dwelling in which God lives by his Spirit.
(Ephesians 2:11-22)

In a nutshell, this reminds Gentiles of the enormous privilege they have to be invited to the party, latecomers without pedigree but with equal standing to the Jews, thanks to the cross. Jesus shed his blood equally for Jew and Gentile and the two were now one, *One New Man*. That's the theory of it anyway.

In practice it has *never* happened. Ever since the first Jewish Christians – the first disciples, Paul, James and the rest – passed from history the Church had become almost completely Gentile and, thanks to the influence of pagan Greek philosophy, gradually managed to rid itself of all Jewish elements. This may seem extreme but then we need to understand the logical effect of Platonic ideas, particularly the effect of a 2nd Century heresy, *Marcionism*, that has never left us. It fed from the *dualism* of Plato that declared that the physical world was evil and the spiritual world good.

This aberration created untold havoc in the thoughts and practices of the Church ever since (for more on this read "How the Church Lost The Way") and Marcionism promoted the idea that the Jews were the physical, rejected and evil people of the *Old* Testament whereas the (Gentile) Christians were the spiritual, chosen and holy people of the *New* Testament. A development of this is what is now known as *Replacement Theology*, where theologians run hither and thither brandishing "proof texts" to back up an idea that had its roots in pagan philosophy and which, not always intentionally, feeds the antisemitism and anti-Israelism (the same thing actually, though more politically correct) that still plagues our Church.

And how is this relevant to today's Christian? Acting Hebraically involves every facet of your Christian life and, now that you have an awareness of the Jewish legacy at the heart of our faith, you ought to respond accordingly. We are all in this together, to try and make One New Man a reality. And it's not there yet.

One New Man is currently a lop-sided pipedream. No-one is currently winning here despite the efforts of some to create a *version* of One New Man. The current rise in *Messianic* fellowships is one such effort. I am not dismissing this trend, it's just I feel that, if One New Man is ever going to arise from the Body of Christ, it is going to have to make an impact in mainstream churches and not around the edges.

Messianic fellowships are a welcome part of the process and address the needs of many Jews and Gentiles willing to go deeper into their faith, but I think they are still interim, a work-in-process, the best fit but by no means the *only* fit. They address the missing Jewish elements, but quite often are consequently as lop-sided (in the opposite direction) as the Gentile Church has been for all those years when *Jewish elements* were surgically removed.

More to the point, how could One New Man ever work? There's a lot of bad history to deal with for starters, lots of repenting and changed attitudes certainly, though not to the extent of Gentiles repenting for every individual act of "Christian" antisemitism in the past, as if they were somehow individually responsible. That is about as ill-advised as condemning the Jews throughout history for the acts of those in Jesus' day – though it didn't stop thousands of Jews being killed and persecuted as "Christ-killers" by the Church over the last 2000 years!

Also, deep, deep down, there's still some resentment and fear, though it is rarely expressed. The resentment is from a smug "certainty" that in Christ we are all equal, so what right do the Jews have claiming some divine importance.

There is neither Jew nor Greek, slave nor free, male nor female, for you are all one in Christ Jesus.
(Galatians 3:28)

Yes, as *individuals*, there is no difference; all need Christ for their personal salvation. An individual Jew is only saved *once*, just like the rest of you; there is no favouritism beyond that.

But Paul specifically speaks of Jews as a people, in a future sense, whether we like it or not, whether it fits into the neat theological solutions that we have bought into, whether your pastor, teacher or minister agrees with it or not. There's no way of reading Romans Chapter 9-11 in any other way, which is why most churches *never* preach on these verses.

> *I do not want you to be ignorant of this mystery, brothers, so that you may not be conceited: Israel has experienced a hardening in part until the full number of the Gentiles has come in. And so all Israel will be saved, as it is written: "The deliverer will come from Zion; he will turn godlessness away from Jacob."*
> (Romans 11:25-26)

This is clearly, unambiguously the *future* and it's a time when many (perhaps all?) Jews are going to return to God. It's a mystery, as it says, so there's no point over-analysing it other than allowing the plain sense of the words to sink in. **God tells us that the Jews, *as a people*, do have a future**.

Israel's hardening is one thing, but what of the Gentile's *hardening* against Israel (the Jews)? This needs to end if One New Man is ever to become a reality and the Church is to enter a time of blessing the like of which perhaps it has never had before. I already touched on one aspect of this in an earlier chapter, when considering this verse, in the context of the great learning and insights orthodox Jews could offer the Church, once they have discovered their Jewish Messiah, *Yeshua*.

> *For if their rejection is the reconciliation of the world, what will their acceptance be but life from the dead?*
> (Romans 11:15)

I mentioned resentment being a barrier, but I also mentioned *fear*. This fear is a fear of going backwards, of being dragged back to the rigid rules and regulations that typified life in the Old Testament times for the Jews. The trigger words are *legalism* and *judaising,* with also much negativity attached to that most maligned and misunderstood word, *Torah,* the law of Moses (better understood as the *teachings* of Moses).

It's one of the really big debates in the Christian world. As *people of grace* what do we do about the *Law,* the Torah, the Old Testament? There's one point of agreement on this issue shared by Gentile believers and Jewish believers and that is ... *there is so little agreement.* The Gentile fear is that these Jewish *Messianic* believers want to impose Torah on all Christians, but this is unfounded as in the Messianic world there is a whole spectrum of different opinions on what to do about Torah.

Some say that the Torah is totally done away with and the only laws that should be upheld are those endorsed within the teachings of Jesus. For these Jewish believers, such things as Sabbath observance and kosher dietary laws are not obligations, though individuals are free to do as their conscience dictates. Others declare that Jesus has adapted the Torah in a New Testament context, even making allowances for the Gentiles. Others cherry-pick which parts of the Torah are still in operation (the moral code) and which aren't (the practical instructions and ceremonial laws). Still others declare the Torah, the whole Torah and nothing but the Torah for Messianic believers in Jesus.

Perhaps we should let Jewish believers thrash out these points among themselves. What we should focus on are the implications of *One New Man* for Gentile Christians. What should their position be in relation to the Torah, the Laws of Moses?

This is where it gets a bit fuzzy. The Ten commandments are part of the Torah, yet many Christians quote them as integral to their code for living and there's more than one group out there using them as discussion starters for evangelism. Are they *under the Law,* then and what do they do about the 4th commandment in its original context, the Saturday Sabbath? So is it valid for Christians to keep the Ten Commandments? What about the other 603 commandments within the first five books of the Old Testament? What about the

Proverbs? What about the Psalms? What about the general principles that underpin the great narratives of the Old Testament, David and Goliath, David and Bathsheba, Noah's Ark, the reasons for the Exile and countless others? Then there are the prophets. How much of what they say can the Church own and apply to itself?

It's a bit of a minefield and not something that can be analysed in depth here. Instead I propose looking at this matter through our *Hebraic* glasses. Firstly we must consider the effect of Greek thinking on matters of law and grace.

Earlier, I mentioned the heresy *Marcionism*, which declared the Old Testament and its people (and its God) physical and evil and the New Testament, spiritual and good. This type of thinking, born out of the dualism of Plato, is still with us in diluted form. The fact that we call the Hebrew Scriptures the *Old* Testament imparts a sense of something done away with, irrelevant and of no use to modern *New Testament* Christians. Many of today's Christians have no use for the Old Testament, except as a source of nice stories and lessons that "may or may not be actually historically true".

Along with this dualism came the Greek propensity for neat classifications, clever divisions that appeal to the analytical mind, nice and neat and tidy. Out of this has come the idea that the Old Testament is all about *law* and the New Testament is all about *grace*. There are two problems with this. There's plenty of grace – undeserved divine favour – in the Old Testament.

Then the word of the LORD came to Elijah the Tishbite: "Have you noticed how Ahab has humbled himself before me? Because he has humbled himself, I will not bring this disaster in his day ...
(1 Kings 21:28-29)

And when he prayed to him, the LORD was moved by his entreaty and listened to his plea; so he brought him back to Jerusalem and to his kingdom. Then Manasseh knew that the LORD is God.
(2 Chronicles 33:13)

When God saw what they (people of Nineveh) did and how they
turned from their evil ways, he had compassion and did not bring
upon them the destruction he had threatened.
(Jonah 3:10)

And there's plenty of law (commandments) in the New Testament.

Anyone who breaks one of the least of these commandments and
teaches others to do the same will be called least in the kingdom
of heaven, but whoever practises and teaches these commands
will be called great in the kingdom of heaven.
(Matthew 5:19)

"Why do you ask me about what is good?" Jesus replied.
"There is only One who is good. If you want to enter life, obey
the commandments."
(Matthew 19:17)

Whoever has my commands and obeys them, he is the one who
loves me. He who loves me will be loved by my Father, and I too
will love him and show myself to him.
(John 14:21)

God is so messy! Why can't He appeal to our logical nature and do
things all neat and tidy? He doesn't because He chooses not to. The
closest we are ever going to understand Him is to train ourselves to
think *Hebraically*.

There's law and grace in both the Old and New Testaments because
we need to view the Bible as one complete whole, with one Author,
who provides us with laws to live by, whether the Torah in the Hebrew
Scriptures (Old Testament), which had the purpose of preserving and
protecting the Jews, or the Laws of Jesus in the New Covenant, which
have the purpose of providing Christians with guidelines to live by.

Without grace in the Hebrew Scriptures there would be no
Hebrew Scriptures, or New Testament, or Bible, or Christians.

If we had survived until the 21st Century it would be as pagans or Jedi warriors! This is because grace was needed to ensure the Old Testament Israelites weren't deservedly wiped out every time they messed up. The covenants of God, His promises to Noah, Abraham, Moses and David, were nothing less than products of His divine grace.

Without law in the New Testament we would have absolutely no rudder to guide us along life's stormy seas. *But we're people of the Spirit*, you cry, *we're free from the yoke of the Law*. Does that mean that we Christians are lawless and proud of it? We must be careful what we say and how we act.

Of course we follow laws, or at least we are meant to. Did you know that, apart from the Sabbath laws, Jesus reiterated all the rest of the Ten Commandments, often expanding on them.

> *You have heard that it was said to the people long ago, 'Do not murder, and anyone who murders will be subject to judgment.' But I tell you that anyone who is angry with his brother will be subject to judgment.*
> (Matthew 5:21-22)

> *You have heard that it was said, 'Do not commit adultery.' But I tell you that anyone who looks at a woman lustfully has already committed adultery with her in his heart.*
> (Matthew 5:27-28)

The Gospels and Letters are full of instructions for us. Does that make us legalists, even if many of these instructions are derived from the Torah of the Old Testament or even some "Traditions of the Elders"? Of course not.

In fact, the Greek mind is very open to laws and regulations and would probably be quite at home with the full set of Torah regulations. Consider the best selling Christian book, *The Purpose Driven Life*. It's a set of rules and regulations to follow on a "40 day spiritual journey" and has sold over 30 million copies.

There are plenty of others of that ilk, as well as seminar and study programmes giving you "x steps in order to achieve y". Our Greek minds love this stuff. Deep down we all like to be told how to do things by others, even if it entails following a detailed programme of do's and dont's.

The Hebraic mind says this: *God, you are at the centre of my life. I thank You for the grace that flows out from You and enables me to follow the laws that You have provided me with to live a godly life of service to You and others. Help me to read Your Bible and act accordingly.*

Yes, we need God to help us, but we also need each other. Over the past two years, Monica and I have travelled all over the country promoting my latest books. This was a new experience for me as I previously thought that a writer's job was finished when the final draft was sent to the printers. Hadn't I heard of the magic word, "marketing"? Apparently not, which was why I hardly sold any books ☹. Anyway, we have visited many churches, Messianic fellowships, conferences and house meetings and, if there's one single over-riding impression, it is this: *there is a growing hunger for authentic, uncompromising Biblical teaching.* People want to go deeper, further than their church experience is taking them. It may be that their church has meandered into a swampy marshland of blandness or error, or just reached a dead-end. If so, then it's every Christian's personal responsibility to either jump ship, stay put and hope for a miracle or go foraging in the hope that they can bring back some tasty morsels (or preferably some juicy steak) to feed the chicks who have stayed behind.

Most folk we met had opted for the latter choice and they have decided that the best places to find this extra depth were meetings where the "Hebrew Roots" of Christianity were being explored. And there's the rub, because this kind of teaching is not welcome in many churches, for reasons given at the head of this chapter. *Too Jewish! We're not having any of that Judaism in my Church!* I believe that these folk are driven by fear, fed by ignorance of the reality of the situation, which is this: *to move deeper into your faith you need to move back to when the Bible was the centre of it, rather than forwards to a Christianity that is being sucked further and further into the World.* And that means returning to the times of Bible folk, who just happen to be Jews. We must work together to remove this fear, that is the point of One New Man, after all.

We have so far discovered such groups in Leicester, Nottingham, Preston, Lincoln, London (all parts), Gateshead, Cambridge, Exmouth and Oxford (if I've missed any out, please forgive me!). If you want details of these groups please email me and I'll put you in touch. If you live elsewhere and feel so led, then email me anyway and I'll try to co-ordinate some way that like-minded folk can fellowship together as they go deeper.

So, *One New Man.* Rather than dwelling on our perceived differences let's just focus on Him who holds it all together.

For there is no difference between Jew and Gentile – the same Lord is Lord of all and richly blesses all who call on him, for, "Everyone who calls on the name of the Lord will be saved."
(Romans 10:12-13)

Bind Us Together

I have a memory of my first church, of particular services led by an ebullient African pastor. He was naive enough to believe that when the first chords of the chorus "Bind us together" were strummed we English-folk would be glad to join hands across the pews in a teeth-grinding (in my case) show of Christian love and togetherness. I have hated that song ever since. Confession over, forgiveness sought and given, so now we move on.

Some of my best friends are Christians. So are a few of my Moriarty's, my Bluto's, my Lex Luthor's (unpack that lot of cultural references, if you will). It's a shameful confession but a reality for many Christians. We get on with most of our Christian brothers and sisters, but there are a few we just don't hit it off with and even one of two whom we wish would … go to a different church! It doesn't end there, certainly not for me, as there are some prominent Christians strutting their stuff out there who, speaking plainly, make my blood boil!

This can't be right, can it? After all:

A new command I give you: Love one another. As I have loved you, so you must love one another. By this all men will know that you are my disciples, if you love one another.
(John 13:34-35)

Surely there must be a loophole somewhere? If there's ever a case for good honest scripture-twisting then this is it! Perhaps the context may help ...

It was at the Last Supper and Judas has just slunk off. Jesus was telling his disciples that he would soon be off to a place where they could not follow. Then he quoted the above verse, telling them to love one another. The next voice heard was Peter's. He had a bee in his bonnet; he wanted to know more about where Jesus was going and was only stopped in his stride by Jesus' prediction of his coming betrayal. The point being made here is that Peter didn't query Jesus' pronouncement about loving one another, so we can assume they were already doing this stuff.

So the mark of a disciple of Jesus is meant to be the love we show for each other. If *every* disciple of Jesus showed such love to every other disciple of Jesus, perhaps we would really start to show the World that *there's something different about these people*.

Paul had more to say on this subject.

As a prisoner for the Lord, then, I urge you to live a life worthy of the calling you have received. Be completely humble and gentle; be patient, bearing with one another in love. Make every effort to keep the unity of the Spirit through the bond of peace.
(Ephesians 4:1-3)

Here's the deal. We disciples of Jesus must show our love for each other in humility, gentleness and patience as a good witness and for the sake of unity. Now's there's unity and there's *Unity*. The Church of England has unity issues over the subject of women priests, over the issue of whether women have the mandate to represent Christ in their sacred rites. Well, this is a Greek issue, a result of Platonism, and a non-starter really as *neither men nor women should* represent Christ, as we *all* have access to Our Lord!

But it must never be unity at any cost. For there to be true Christian unity, it has to be based on truth. Sometimes, this is in short supply in the Christian World and there are some fellow brothers and sisters who really try our gentleness and patience, who perhaps provoke us to many ungodly thoughts.

Now, as someone working in the Christian media, I have had a chance to examine many prominent and influential ministries and I must confess that there are many dangerous Christians out there who tread a fine line on what is acceptable in terms of doctrine and/or behaviour. Two words that cry out to me are *carnality* and *heresy*, worldliness and bad theology. Do I really share a faith with people who promote prosperity or false prophecy or deny basic core principles of the faith? Are they *really* my brothers and sisters?

And there's the rub. Who are my brothers and sisters? We are meant to show love and unity, but what about discernment?

Watch out for false prophets. They come to you in sheep's clothing, but inwardly they are ferocious wolves.
(Matthew 7:15)

This is a difficult one because not everything is as it seems. Believe it or not, not everyone who claims to be Christian *is* one. How do we discern this? Well, Scripture helps here. Let's read the rest of the passage in Matthew.

By their fruit you will recognise them. Do people pick grapes from thornbushes, or figs from thistles? Likewise every good tree bears good fruit, but a bad tree bears bad fruit. A good tree cannot bear bad fruit, and a bad tree cannot bear good fruit. Every tree that does not bear good fruit is cut down and thrown into the fire. Thus, by their fruit you will recognise them. "Not everyone who says to me, 'Lord, Lord,' will enter the kingdom of heaven, but only he who does the will of my Father who is in heaven. Many will say to me on that day, 'Lord, Lord, did we not prophesy in your name, and in your name drive out demons and perform many miracles?' Then I will tell them plainly, 'I never knew you. Away from me, you evildoers!'
(Matthew 7:16-23)

The heart of this is the frightening statement:

Not everyone who says to me, 'Lord, Lord,' will enter the kingdom of heaven, but only he who does the will of my Father who is in heaven.

It is clear that the mark of a Christian is not what he says, but what he *does*. So many folk know the lingo, can talk the talk, can give every impression they have regenerated hearts, but have they really? Just like the *sophists* of Ancient Greece, professional orators paid for their work, some are earning a nice living in the Christian world, particularly the media. Judging by the techniques used to fleece the flock and promote highly dubious theologies, it is highly unlikely that these folk have a real relationship with the Lord Jesus. The Matthew passage reminds us:

By their fruit you will recognise them.

This is important because, without any evidence of a regenerated heart, a life given over to God, the probability is that there is *no* regenerated heart.

Some people are Christians by name only, deluding themselves. For this, I put the blame on Greek thinking. When I was first introduced to Jesus, I accepted his claims on an intellectual level quite quickly. It made sense to me, even as I delved into the history and theology. I knew that Jesus was *theoretically* my saviour. I had a very *Greek* salvation, head knowledge, not heart knowledge. If I had died before this revelation had reached my heart then all this knowledge would have been absolutely no use to me. Theory doesn't save souls, only practice does, making a decision of the will to allow the Holy Spirit to enter my life, sweep me clean of the rubbish and lift me up and partner with me on the greatest journey anyone can go on.

How many out there have a Greek salvation, who see their Christian convictions as just a system of philosophy, a source of good argument at dinner parties, a guarded position in heated debates? A Jesus of the mind but not the heart. If this is you, then get *Hebraic*, get on your knees and make the decision to allow Jesus to inform your actions and conduct and not just your thoughts.

So, what about Christian unity? Let's remind ourselves:

A new command I give you: Love one another. As I have loved you, so you must love one another. By this all men will know that you are my disciples, if you love one another.
(John 13:34-35)

As a prisoner for the Lord, then, I urge you to live a life worthy of the calling you have received. Be completely humble and gentle; be patient, bearing with one another in love. Make every effort to keep the unity of the Spirit through the bond of peace.
(Ephesians 4:1-3)

Firstly, we have to be clear about *who are* our Christian brothers and sisters, disciples of Jesus. There can be no unity of the Spirit if we're *not all* following the same Spirit. Unity for unity's sake is no good unless it is undergirded by the truth. We have to get real here and consider that, as ever, the World is watching us. If we condone and support ministries that are *clearly from another planet*, then it makes us all look stupid and gullible and diminishes the Gospel.

Unfortunately, many Christians are gullible. Our fellowship certainly was when we actually ran evening meetings to plan for the "inevitable collapse of society" as a result of the millennium bug in 2000. How stupid did we look afterwards and what good did that do for the Gospel? What about those who follow prophets who are declared false by the mere fact that specific prophecies don't come to pass? Do we stone them as false prophets? No, we carry on funding them and following them because we look up to them, we want them to be right eventually, otherwise we'd look foolish. Wake up! You have already demonstrated foolishness by your actions. What good did that do for the Gospel?

Of course most deception is more subtle than this.

But there were also false prophets among the people, just as there will be false teachers among you. They will secretly introduce destructive heresies, even denying the sovereign Lord who bought them – bringing swift destruction on themselves. Many will follow their shameful ways and will bring the way of truth into disrepute. In their greed these teachers will exploit you with stories they have made up. Their condemnation has long been hanging over them, and their destruction has not been sleeping.
(2 Peter 2:1-3)

This could be today's headline. These people are among us and we need to get back to our Bibles and refute them, marginalise them and publicly reject them for the sake of true Christian unity. They claim to be Christian but their words and actions condemn them. Don't listen uncritically to their words, but be like the Bereans.

Now the Bereans were of more noble character than the Thessalonians, for they received the message with great eagerness and examined the Scriptures every day to see if what Paul said was true.
(Acts 17:11)

Watch their actions, particularly the shenanigans *off-camera*. What sort of lives are they leading, how are their marriages, what do they say in their unscripted, unguarded moments? Remember ...

Watch out for false prophets. They come to you in sheep's clothing, but inwardly they are ferocious wolves.
(Matthew 7:15)

We are called to love our fellow Christian brothers and sisters for the sake of unity but without compromise. What this means in reality is that we must show love for all *true* brothers and sisters in Christ, even if we need to show humility because of *secondary* theological differences, gentleness to those with whom we are unfamiliar and patience for those whom we would normally find quite challenging.

A friend was telling me about meetings he took part in, to plan for a huge mission in his town. The interesting point was that those present were from a complete spectrum of the Christian world, from ultra-charismatics who hear from God every few minutes to older folk from Brethren backgrounds, with very firm reservations about spiritual gifts. What was special about this meeting was that, because the focus was on worshipping Jesus and reaching the lost, all differences were irrelevant. What bound them together as Christian brothers and sisters was stronger than what divided them, in doctrinal differences. Action outweighed words.

Instead, speaking the truth in love, we will in all things grow up into him who is the Head, that is, Christ. From him the whole body, joined and held together by every supporting ligament, grows and builds itself up in love, as each part does its work.
(Ephesians 4:15-16)

We tend to think very parochially, a result of the chopping up of the Body of Christ into congregation-sized portions, each with a geographical sphere of influence. If we could see the big picture, this spiritual being with Christ at its head, the *Church* rather than individual churches, then it would be easier for us to accept each other as fellow, functional members of the Body.

To each *true* brother and sister we must show demonstrable love for the sake of the Gospel. In my case it means loving those who have embraced replacement theology, as well as the Anglican vicar down the road with whom I have absolutely nothing in common (apart from a love of Jesus). You will of course have your own set of challenges.

Calvinists and Arminians will need to start talking to each other again. Christian Zionists and Supercessionists will have to conduct their public debates without emotion or recrimination. Theistic evolutionists and Creationists will need to stop sneering at each other. Reformers and (born again) Catholics will have to kiss and make up. All for the sake of the Gospel.

And why do we do it? It is because Jesus commands us to do so and I believe blessing will come to us as a result. *By this all men will know that you are my disciples.* After all, isn't that what it's all about?

Intermission #3: Acting Hebraically.

It's all very well living our lives Hebraically by getting our relationships right and thinking Hebraically by relying on God to provide for all of our needs, but the bottom line is what we do with all these blessings. Do we keep a tight hold of them, thanking God profusely but shielding them from the outside World? Or do we show the World, by the way that we interact with it, the love of God that glows in our heart?

We don't have a jealously guarded secret, we have a great commission to fulfil:

> *Therefore go and make disciples of all nations, baptising them in the name of the Father and of the Son and of the Holy Spirit, and teaching them to obey everything I have commanded you. And surely I am with you always, to the very end of the age.*
> (Matthew 28:19-20)

The best way of making disciples is by showing what a good disciple you are and teaching them to do likewise. It's our actions, perhaps more than our words, that are going to speak most into folks' hearts. So it's time to break free of the negative stereotypes that have plagued us for so long, the accusations of self-righteousness, coldness and lack of humour and start to trumpet the joy within us:

> *For the kingdom of God is not a matter of eating and drinking, but of righteousness, peace and joy in the Holy Spirit.*
> (Romans 14:17)

Is this what people see when they see you? Or do they see a Holy Joe, brandishing his Bible like a cudgel and his tongue like a rapier? It is time folk recognised Christians by their *righteousness, peace and joy in the Holy Spirit*, rather than by their long faces and ready sneers. It's time we were seen as being *different*, something not currently borne out by sociological surveys.

We must also endeavour to right a wrong that has disgraced the Church since almost the very beginning, our attitude to the Jewish people. Acquaint yourself with the history of the Church in terms of its conduct to the Jews and you will understand why they are so resistant to the Gospel. God still loves them, He hasn't forgotten His promises to them, although the Church largely has. Buck the trend and try to make a difference and God will surely bless you. When the *One New Man* of Ephesians 2 finally materialises, all will be blessed and only then, I believe, can the Church experience true release.

A final word on Christian unity. Strive for it but never at the expense of truth. There's a fifth column among us, destroying us from within by blackening the real Gospel of Jesus Christ. They follow a *different Gospel* and we need to avoid them at all costs.

For if someone comes to you and preaches a Jesus other than the Jesus we preached, or if you receive a different spirit from the one you received, or a different gospel from the one you accepted, you put up with it easily enough.
(2 Corinthians 11:4)

There's only one way of doing this. Get into the Word of God, soak yourself in it and allow it to cleanse you from all the filth and falsehood that has attached itself to your dark places. Be like the *Bereans* and learn to use the Word of God to inform the way you see the World and discern truth from error.

Acting Hebraically is when we put all the theory into practice and live lives of truth, joy and purpose, prompting the World to exclaim *we want what they have and we want it now!*

Just Do It!

It struck me that, by dividing this last section – The Life – into three parts, each an aspect of *doing it Hebraically*, I have succumbed to the same Greek thought that divides everything up and classifies it into neat little boxes. So we need to be holistic about this and realise that living, thinking and acting Hebraically should flow naturally together; we ought to live in godly relationships, with our thinking resulting in godly actions. It's a complete package, which of course the Christian deal was always meant to be.

> *But we ought always to thank God for you, brothers loved by the Lord, because from the beginning God chose you to be saved through the sanctifying work of the Spirit and through belief in the truth. He called you to this through our gospel, that you might share in the glory of our Lord Jesus Christ. So then, brothers, stand firm and hold to the teachings we passed on to you, whether by word of mouth or by letter. May our Lord Jesus Christ himself and God our Father, who loved us and by his grace gave us eternal encouragement and good hope, encourage your hearts and strengthen you in every good deed and word.*
> (2 Thessalonians 2:13-17)

So, here are some thoughts, ideas and suggestions to throw into the mix. The first thing that comes to mind is the real harm done by Greek thinking.

Consider Mr Smartypants. He is theologically astute, knows his interpretations of his Bible inside out and is willing to lock horns intellectually with anyone who dares to see the Bible any differently. He is not for turning, as he has invested much time and effort in reaching his positions and is not going to allow any argument, however eloquently stated, to sway him. This rigidity has its origins in Greek thinking and indeed was a prominent feature of the Christian world during the time of the Church Fathers. It's a tendency to see Christianity as a philosophy rather than a living faith and fights its battles in the mental realm, with lots of hot air but very little fruit and sadly very little concern for the effects of these views. An example is the Replacement Theology that is the UK church's prominent argument for the relationship between the Church and Israel. The effects of these views have historically given rise to a very negative view of Jewish people, resulting in some of the most shameless actions ever conducted by the Church in the name of God. Another example is those Christians who are so bursting with anticipation and excitement over the rapture or second coming of Christ, yet seem oblivious to the issue of the billions of human beings who will be left in the tribulation or shipped off to Hell.

Then there's Miss Fluffypants. She's been sold on the idea that God is so loveable that He is willing to allow everyone into Heaven, as long as they are sincerely following their particular path, even if Jesus is absent from this path. *How could a loving God consign anyone to Hell*, she argues, though her view of this place is a far cry from the way Jesus described it in the Gospels. Her view of God is coloured by sentimentality, encouraged by liberal thinking that was born out of Greek rationalism. She has recreated God in her own imagination as an acceptable, reasonable, fluffy God. This is *not* the God of the Bible, the sovereign, Almighty God of justice who reminds us that only Jesus provides the ticket to everlasting life and the alternative ain't pretty!

Jesus answered, "I am the way and the truth and the life. No one comes to the Father except through me."
(John 14:6)

Finally there's Mr Gracepants, who has inherited an incorrect understanding that relegates everything that smacks of Law to the cobweb-strewn unopened drawer of the Old Testament and insists that, as a people of grace, we're pretty much free to do what we want, *as the Spirit moves us*. We have already seen that there's plenty of grace in the Old Testament and that, despite what many Christians think, we are *still* under the law, *Jesus' law*. This wrong thinking is born out of the *dualism* of Plato, which tends to divide and conquer us, setting up imagined conflicts between soul versus body, sacred versus secular, clergy versus laity and law versus grace.

So we need a correct view of God, His word and how to express this faith that burns within. We need to be living, thinking and acting Hebraically, all three. Think how this can affect us in how we live our lives.

Let's think about evangelism, God's command to us to *go and make disciples of all nations*. (Matthew 28:19). Mr Smartypants would try to argue someone into the Kingdom, Miss Fluffypants would promise warm fuzziness and the assurance of a life without pain and hardship and Mr Gracepants would offer us a fast-track to heaven with no restrictions in this life.

How should we reach out to the unsaved, then? Not speaking as an expert, or offering a quick-fit solution, it seems clear that it's not just what we say, but how we say it and how we live our lives. We need to be able to back up our words with a living understanding, not just a head knowledge, of God and His scriptures, but we also need to be able to demonstrate a changed life, evidence of the Holy Spirit living in us. Philosophy can't deliver you from life-long habits, only Jesus can. Good works may give you a sense of value, but won't get you to Heaven, only Jesus can.

Our relationship to God needs to be consciously holistic. Prayer needs to become as natural as breathing or talking. Of course, God is a spiritual being, but we don't need to be in "spiritual" places to speak to Him, or even being in a "spiritual" mood (otherwise many of us may never get to speak to Him!) This is not to say that we ought to be over-familiar to the extent of taking Him for granted, but simply to say that conversation and interaction is the oxygen for any developing relationship. You can *never* say too much to God, though of course we must make room for anything *He* may want to contribute to the conversation. And never forget *Who* you are speaking to; you may sometimes be irrelevant but you should *never* be irreverent.

Our worship should always simply be our individual response to the awesomeness of God and the incredible gift of salvation that He has given us. It's not just something you do in response to the promptings of a worship leader. You can worship God with everything that is you, not just your singing voice. You can cry out to Him in exaltation; you can also worship Him in your creativity. Many moons ago I dedicated my writing talent to His Kingdom and since then I have always seen my writing efforts as my acts of worship. Your gifting may be different, perhaps through art, or pottery, or dance, or even sporting prowess. Give it all back to Him with a thankful attitude and that would be acceptable to the One who gave you these gifts. God has created us as mind, body and spirit and it is surely right for us to worship Him in mind, body and spirit.

We have been indoctrinated into the idea of this Greek secular/ sacred divide, this separation of our lives into two compartments labelled, 'this is me in Christian mode' and 'this is me everywhere else'. For too long many Christians have considered the two hours in the church building *in my Sunday best clothes and behaviour* as sufficient to earn brownie-points for Heaven, as the minimum entry-level requirement. This barrier needs to be consciously broken down by every Christian so that we truly live our lives 24/7 for God, as His missionaries to wherever He has put you. As churches we may send out missionaries to far-flung places, with promises of financial and prayer support, but we must consider ourselves too as missionaries to our school, our office, our family, our friends, our neighbours. It's a battle-ground out there and many of us are defeated before we've even got started, because we're not sure *how* to get started. The World is becoming a more and more frightening place for Christians, due to the relentless secularisation of western society and we need to be guided by what the Bible says. How are we meant to interact with the World?

(Jesus speaking) I have given them your word and the world has hated them, for they are not of the world any more than I am of the world. My prayer is not that you take them out of the world but that you protect them from the evil one. They are not of the world, even as I am not of it. Sanctify them by the truth; your word is truth. As you sent me into the world, I have sent them into the world.
(John 17:14-18)

We are sent into the World, guided by God's truth, the Bible. We are to be salt and light and a bright shining witness, but we also need to know how far we can go, before we are sucked into the World's ways and our witness diluted to such an extent that there is little difference between us and them.

You adulterous people, don't you know that friendship with the world is hatred toward God? Anyone who chooses to be a friend of the world becomes an enemy of God.
(James 4:4)

This is surely one of the most frightening Scripture verses for those of us Christians who feel called to be witnesses within our western culture, whether it's in the media, the arts, education, the legal system, science or politics. If our friendship leads to compromise, then we are not representing God in truth and have become *an enemy of God.* One way to ensure this doesn't happen is to live, think and act Hebraically. That means our witness is not just what we say, but must be visibly undergirded by good relationships, good theology and good conduct. Then non-believers may disagree with what we are saying, because God's truth will challenge them in uncomfortable ways, but at least they will see that we are living our lives in a way that is consistent with our message.

Finally, just stop and think for a bit. As I've said time and time again in this book, these are not new revelations, just a nudge to get us back to a *Biblical* way of doing things, so that we can give back to God the very best that we have.

We are therefore Christ's ambassadors, as though God were making his appeal through us. We implore you on Christ's behalf: Be reconciled to God.
(2 Corinthians 5:20)

Be good ambassadors.

CHAPTER

18

To Life!

It's a merry gathering. Glasses are lifted up, chinked together to the accompaniment of *cheers, bottoms up, prost, na zdorovje, salut, chin chin or santé,* all declaring good health or something meaningless. When a Jew lifts up a glass it's *l'chaim,* to life!

To life! What a declaration! As mentioned earlier, the Hebraic way is of movement, of emotion, of power, of life! Life is important, we only get one chance at it; there are few things sadder than a wasted life. To the medieval Church, riddled with Greek nonsense, life was just a stepping stone to the after-life, of little value except to secure a good passage to the next World. But to the *Hebraic* mind, God created the body and the soul as complementary, not the deadly enemies that Plato falsely presumed them to be, and so life is to be valued and enjoyed as a God-given blessing. Jesus agreed with this:

I have come that they may have life and have it to the full.
(John 10:10)

There is enough Greek residue in the modern Church to dent our expectations for true joy and openness to blessings. The more we view every part of our existence with Hebraic eyes, the more work God can do with us to mould us and shape us into the likeness of Jesus. This ought to be the goal of every Christian and we are all at different points in the journey, I fully acknowledge that my wife, Monica, is much further along the road than I am.

Of course, you don't need an understanding of the Hebraic mindset to achieve this, as many are Hebraic without even realising it. This is not surprising as to be Hebraic is simply to be Biblical and many have managed to live true Biblical lives by studying the Bible and all that it has to say rather than living second-hand Christian lives through Church traditions and the mistaken understandings brought about through Greek thinking.

We have met the first Church in the early part of this book and marvelled at its life and vitality, realising that the meagre descriptions provided by Acts and the Letters are but a mere sumptuous snapshot of a people *acting*, *thinking* and *living* truly Hebraically (Biblically), in full relationship with God and each other. It was a true *Biblical Church*.

Then came the Greeks with their hierarchies and systems and pagan philosophies and the slippery slope downwards from the house meetings of those small groups, living in power and truth, to the cold, massive edifices, the churches and cathedrals, built to propagate an ecclesiastical system which served only to separate man from God.

So what do we do? Can we really strip out all alien influences or, like the parable of the weeds, do we wait for the final harvest and leave it to God's mercy? I believe we *can* turn the clocks back, in fact it is our duty to seek out Bible truth and act accordingly. Some folk have tried and failed, others claim it *can't* be done, saying that the first Church was a unique one-time phenomenon and, when it had served its purpose, God broke the mould and cranked everything down a notch or two. Perhaps people who hold that view are reacting, quite rightly, to the excesses and corruptions of the historical Church, particularly in the area of spiritual gifts and anointings. But this is not the whole story …

Because God always has a faithful remnant; that's how He has always worked, from Bible times onwards. Pockets of Biblical Christianity remained separated from the mainstream Greek/

Roman Church from quite early times, including the Celtic Church in Britain, the Waldenses in Europe and the Paulicians in Asia. All were opposed and eventually persecuted by the Catholic Church. There was an intriguing progression from the English reformer John Wycliffe, to the European Hussites and Moravians, then back to England with John Wesley and the Methodists. It is telling that the Methodists, as already mentioned, were notable for their Hebraic nature, with their accent on holiness, doctrine and simple structures. Since then, there has continued to be a faithful remnant, folk from all denominations who are true disciples of the Lord Jesus Christ, despite their exposure to the toxic Greek trappings.

Of course, you don't have to have a knowledge or understanding of the Hebraic mindset to be a true disciple of the Lord Jesus Christ and most haven't a clue about this Hebraic/Greek conflict. It's not a *salvation* issue, but it is a *blessings* issue. The closer we get to the Hebraic, Biblical mindset, the more God can bless us. Let us now remind ourselves what this mindset is.

Two passages in James are a help here:

If any of you lacks wisdom, he should ask God, who gives generously to all without finding fault, and it will be given to him. But when he asks, he must believe and not doubt, because he who doubts is like a wave of the sea, blown and tossed by the wind. That man should not think he will receive anything from the Lord; he is a double-minded man, unstable in all he does.
(James 1:5-8)

As the body without the spirit is dead, so faith without deeds is dead.
(James 2:26)

From this we realise that *faith in God underpins our wisdom, which compels us to perform our deeds.* An historical survey then showed us that State Christianity gave us a Church that failed miserably in this regard, its deeds far removed from those expected from born-again believers in Jesus. The fault for this owes its origins to the Greek mindset, particularly with its tendency to place priority on thought rather than correct action. Matthew Arnold, in the 19th Century, summed up the difference between the Greek and Hebrew mindset:

> *The governing idea of Hellenism is spontaneity of consciousness; that of Hebraism, strictness of conscience. Christianity changed nothing in this essential bent of Hebraism to set doing above knowing. Self-conquest, self-devotion, the following not of our own individual will, but the will of God, obedience, is the fundamental idea of this form, also, of the discipline to which we have attached the general name of Hebraism.*

The Gospel of Jesus Christ came from a Hebraic mindset, from Hebrew thinking. The key to the Hebraic mindset is **faith in God** and the result of the Hebraic mindset is the **performing of deeds**. *Faith and works* – working together – they are at the heart of our Christian faith, our *Hebraic* Christian faith. The Greek way is the way of *man*, but the Hebraic way is the Biblical way, is the Christian way, is the way of *God*. The Christian faith is all about God. It is His initiative: God chooses us to become His people. The goal of sanctification is to *become like Jesus* in this life, the goal of justification is *to be with God* in the next life!

But theory is not going to change your life; practical pointers are what is needed. I took the liberty of suggesting nine areas for consideration, where we can see the Hebraic mindset having impact in the way we "do Church". I divided them into three groupings.

The first was *living Hebraically*, focussing on our relationships.

1. Reverence for God

Total respect and unquestioning faith in God in every situation.

2. Small groups

An emphasis on personal relationships within the Church.

3. Family relationships

God's blessings flow freer through His covenant people.

The second was *thinking Hebraically*, focussing on understanding God's provisions for us.

4. Living by faith

Total reliance on God's promises for our needs.

5. Trusting the Bible

Treat God's Word as precious and endeavour to study it wholeheartedly.

6. The real Jesus

Understand Jesus in his Jewish context.

The third was *acting Hebraically*, living lives of truth, joy and purpose.

7. Good conduct

Show the World by our actions that there is something different about us.

8. What about the Jew?

Understanding the concept of One New Man and making adjustments if necessary.

9. Unity without compromise

Supporting our Christian family without condoning error and heresy.

It's just a checklist, it's not a *Hebraic* Nine Commandments, brought by revelation after forty days and nights camping on Pancake Hill (my childhood haunt). Mostly it is stating the obvious and, of course, you may already be dealing with each area in your daily walk. On the other hand, some of it may have touched a nerve or tugged at your spirit. None of us has really got it all totally right, I know I certainly haven't. There's always room for improvement.

The next step is up to you. You may feel the call for a radical change in the way you "do Church", in which case you must act according to your conscience and with the advice of your accountability partners. This is not necessarily a rallying cry for folk to leave their churches and denominations and create yet more churches and denominations, instead it is a cry perhaps for re-evaluation and for Christians to start to make a difference *at the place where God has put them*. If God hasn't clearly told you to move, then you shouldn't move because ... He's the boss. Even if you feel ineffective where you are, it's your responsibility at least to try and make a difference. Here are some suggestions that may help:

◊ Get into the habit of thanking God for all aspects of your life, not with grand worthy prayers but with simple statements, either spoken out loud or not, depending on circumstances. Especially, always thank Him for blessings in your life, however mundane they may seem, like a successful bowel movement, or a kind deed by a stranger. And if your day is particularly uneventful, you can always thank Him for your salvation!

◊ Make sure you are accountable. Find another Christian (preferably of the same sex) who you feel able to share your deepest thoughts and fears with and always have a correctable spirit. Even a small men's group or ladies group could suffice. The point is to stay connected to the Body of Christ at every level.

◊ Find like-minded people for serious Bible Study, perhaps in midweek. I am hoping to address this key subject in my next book.

◊ Trust God just a little bit more than you are at present. Who knows where that may lead?

◊ Never forget that the World watches us, waiting for us to slip up, to give them another excuse to mock God.

◊ Be a good witness out there. This doesn't have to mean evangelising everything that moves, but just being generally helpful, loving, caring, demonstrating the joy that is within you, and doing it all with a smile (*listen to yourself for once, says Monica*). Let's destroy those negative stereotypes once and for all!

◊ Let the World know Christians for the love we have for each other. But, on the other hand, let us show that we will not tolerate heresy and carnality from those who claim to be our brothers and sisters.

◊ If you are not led to a local church – whether a traditional one or a house church – then what could be better than returning to the *original model*, the Biblical Church, perhaps just two or three families meeting and sharing in a living room. This website will be useful for you, www.house-church.org, with an excellent book, *Biblical Church*, by Beresford Job, to help you with the theory and practice.

◊ There may be others in your church or local area who are on a similar journey. There are many groups springing up in the UK who have monthly meetings and special celebrations, to help folk understand more about the Hebraic roots. There will be a directory of such groups on my Saltshakers website www.hebrewroots.com, so that would be a good place to start.

◊ Try to experience a Messianic Passover demonstration, a wonderful faith-builder that appeals to all senses and is a good example of Hebraic lifestyle, as well as providing fantastic insights to the origins of *Holy Communion*. If you have already been to one, why not get together with others and host one yourself. If you want to try and run it yourself, there is an excellent resource, 'Christ our Passover' a DVD by Chris Hill and available from www.clministries.org.uk. If you need others to run it, then Jews for Jesus www.jewsforjesus.org and Messianic Testimony www.messianictestimony.com can help out here.

◊ Think about developing an environment in your home and church where all are able to develop and exercise their own gifts, whatever they are. Here's an idea I proposed in "How the Church lost The Way":

Perhaps it is time we started to look at the Hebraic way of worshipping God. Perhaps we haven't thought big enough when we think of our BIG God. Knowing that He values every part of us, body, mind and spirit, perhaps we should be worshipping Him, *body, mind and spirit*. It's time to think new, to think big. Just imagine the following ... Posters adorn shop fronts, leaflets thrust into unsuspecting hands. A new Christian worship centre is opening up in town. Groans give way to piqued interest as the text of the leaflets doesn't follow the usual script.

Come along to NewTown church and worship God in new ways. Something for everyone and everything for the glory of God. Music, dance, arts & crafts, drama, discussions, writing and poetry classes, Hebrew lessons. Open all hours.

Is worship all about nice songs, ancient and modern? Worship is about all we can give back to God. Worship is about dance, particularly within the framework of modest dress and behaviour. Worship is about study of God's Word, either individually or in discussion and argument. Worship is about the creative arts, writing and performing drama, poetry, prose, pottery or papier mache. Worship is the exercise of all the gifts and talents that God has given you, given back to Him, to bless Him and others. Do we really need specialists to lead us into God's presence? Surely there must be room for a model that involves ALL of God's people, exercising their gifts and talents in a nurturing communal atmosphere, blessing each other and blessing God in the process. Isn't this worship, too? It's worth thinking about, isn't it?

◊ Look for a local group who are actively praying for Israel. *Pray for the peace of Jerusalem: May those who love you be secure.*

(Psalm 122:6). Prayer for Israel, www.prayer4i.org have such groups all over the UK

◊ Visit my websites. *Saltshakers*, www.hebrewroots.com is packed full of articles, sermons, bible studies and chat, all relevant to the material in this book. *Saffron Planet*, www.saffronplanet.net is our family and friends having a good old chat about things that matter. We are told that it is quite entertaining. *Church: Lost and Found*, www.churchlostandfound.com is the website for this series of books, if you want to keep in touch. You may also follow me on Twitter, #biblicalchurch.

◊ Get hold of and read some of the books in the booklist at the end of this book (Yes, I know some of them are mine!) They are all worth reading to help you go deeper.

If I had to condense what being Hebraic is, into a single sentence, it would be this: *unswerving faith in God and His Word and your unconditional response to Him in your thoughts, lives and deeds.* Consider this, you may already be in a good place in your relationship with God and fellow believers and all that flows from it. That's fine, but what if you knew that what is good could be *even better*, that whatever blessings you are currently receiving could be multiplied and multiplied ... ? Isn't that worth going for? Then, what's stopping you ... go for it!

Can we really return to the *original blueprint*, the thriving, exciting, awesome Biblical Church of the first apostles? Can we really? Ought we to try? I believe so, because there is nothing to lose except the most incredible blessings if we don't. And the best chance we have is to train ourselves to think Hebraically, to think Biblically.

And, finally ... this is *not* the final word on the subject, this is just the beginning. If there's one message, there is so much more to say and I pray, by the grace of God, that this is just the start of a fascinating, wonderful, faith-affirming journey deeper into the heart of God for all of us.

Don't analyse it, just do it!

Observation #2: Ten Hebraic things your church could do ...

Just a bit of serious fun, but have a look at this list. Does your church do any of these? Would it be willing to try any of these? Let me know how you get on.

1. **Put the worship group behind the congregation** – the focus must always be on God, but sometimes the group can distract (not necessarily their fault).

2. **Have a sermon Q & A** – does the preacher have the courage of his convictions? Be like the Bereans and query anything that you're not sure about. I'm not preaching anarchy here, just a 10 minute slot that could continue afterwards over a nice cup of tea.

3. **Pray for the Peace of Jerusalem** – Add this to your liturgy (Psalm 122) to show your debt of gratitude for those who have suffered greatly at the hands of the Church. Bless Israel and you will be blessed (Genesis 12:3).

4. **Use matzah (unleavened bread) in your Communion service** – why do we use bread with yeast to represent the body of Christ? Read 1 Corinthians 5:6-8 and think again.

5. **Smash the collection plate** – Trust that the Lord won't allow you to go short and, if folk want to bless you financially, they won't need to be asked.

6. **Re-arrange the seating** – The "pews" system was intentionally designed to emphasise the clergy/laity divide. Allow folk to face each other, with the leaders integrated with the congregation.

7. **Think about Davidic Dance** – Anybody can do it and this type of dancing can generate real joy in a congregation (though may be at odds with point 1. above!)

8. **No preacher days** – perhaps once a month, just have an unstructured service where folk can share – testimonies, bible readings, prayers or observations. A throwback to the original Biblical Church.

9. **Hebrew Word of the Week** – Hebrew words have such an incredible richness of meaning. Find someone willing to introduce a new word every week and show how Jesus fulfilled it in some way, if possible.

10. **Joint services/meetings** – mix and match services with another local church, to emphasise unity and brotherhood within the Body of Christ.

CHAPTER 19

The Crux of the Matter

The title says it all, the crux of the matter, the *cross* of the matter. Actually, the cross *is* the matter, the cross of Jesus, the means by which we can enter the life that God always intended us to have. Although this book is my attempt to define it, promote it and teach it, being Hebraic is not just following clever formulae and check lists, it is an attitude of the heart and we would do well to consider again the familiar Scripture that underpins this book:

> *Jesus answered, "I am the way and the truth and the life. No one comes to the Father except through me.*
> (John 14:6)

Yes, it is a much repeated statement, particularly among us writers, but it is true nevertheless – *it really is all about Jesus.* He is The Life. All we need to do now is to understand *exactly* what that means, without reverting to jargon or cliché.

Firstly, he is the reason and purpose for life.

> *He is the image of the invisible God, the firstborn over all creation. For by him all things were created: things in heaven and on earth, visible and invisible, whether thrones or powers*

or rulers or authorities; all things were created by him and for him.
(Colossians 1:15-16)

Try telling that to the playboy, living a life of pure hedonism or the politician feeding on the power that comes with his position, or even the secular charity worker devoting his life to the wellbeing of others. Without Jesus, all their lives may not be without rewards, but no more than flecks of foam on the surface of a deep, deep ocean. Without Jesus, their lives may have value but will always be marred by the biggest mistake anyone could make, turning down the possibility of an eternity in Heaven.

We belong to him, we are his, all of us who accept the calling.

And you also are among those who are called to belong to Jesus Christ.
(Romans 1:6)

Accepting this calling has implications not just in the afterlife, but in this life too, because Jesus has a promise for us.

I have come that they may have life, and have it to the full.
(John 10:10)

Jesus lived the perfect life, a template that we could never completely fit, though it is our lifelong goal to mould ourselves into the best possible fit.

Now the Lord is the Spirit, and where the Spirit of the Lord is, there is freedom. And we, who with unveiled faces all reflect the Lord's glory, are being transformed into his likeness with ever-increasing glory, which comes from the Lord, who is the Spirit.
(2 Corinthians 3:17-18)

So what does this mean? In a nutshell, it is that we Christians should strive to be *transformed into his likeness*. This is the life that Jesus offers us, a full life in this World, followed by a fuller life in the next. Who would seriously want to turn this offer down?

Sadly most do and though the chief reason is the pride of man to want to live his life *his* way, it is not always helped by the witness of those who have said 'yes' to Jesus.

What do they see in us? Do they see Jesus reflected in our words and particularly in our actions? Do they see a work of transformation into Jesus' likeness or do they see a person who's "gone religious", who has turned judgemental, critical and serious? Where is the life in that? There are too many Christians out there with sour faces and attitudes, who have been sucked into the Greek mindset of viewing their faith simply as a philosophy to be argued over rather than the Hebraic mindset that emphasises a *changed life*.

I will say this again. The life that Jesus wants us to follow is one of transformation into his likeness and it is my contention that only by living, thinking and acting Hebraically, according to the guidance of Holy Scripture, can we do so. It requires effort on our part, a true partnership with the Holy Spirit, who may prompt and teach, but will never take over. Let's not get all super-spiritual about this, you are in the driving seat. It is not just about the supernatural, there is real work to be done by you.

But the fruit of the Spirit is love, joy, peace, patience, kindness, goodness, faithfulness, gentleness and self-control. Against such things there is no law. Those who belong to Christ Jesus have crucified the sinful nature with its passions and desires. Since we live by the Spirit, let us keep in step with the Spirit. Let us not become conceited, provoking and envying each other.
(Galatians 5:22-26)

Keep in step with the Spirit and discover the life that God intended for you.

Sometimes, I just pause and consider what it *really* actually is that we have been freely given. We have the assurance that our lives can have meaning and our pathways through it don't have to be random meanderings. We are promised a destiny – it may not involve the big things that happened to those big characters in the Bible, but if we can just touch one other soul in this life, then joy should follow.

Too many of us Christians are wrapped up in our individual needs. We sometimes even worry about our own salvation, torn between the assurance of a once-saved-always-saved mindset and the need to work out our salvation with fear and trembling (Philippians 2:12). Others have an unhealthy yearning for the Rapture. We don't just worry about such things, but we debate them with other believers and even fall out with each other over them. Personally I trust my Lord to do the very best for me, whether it is to reward me or judge me. I just concentrate on doing my best to fulfil the tasks He gives me to do and leave the rest to Him.

We are not given a free meal ticket, a 'get out of jail free card' in terms of invulnerable bodies or self-replicating bank accounts. We don't have charmed, lucky or fortunate lives, we have blessed ones, blessed not always by physical health and wealth but through the knowledge that we have entered a partnership with God and He will be with us every step of the way.

We have all of this, and yes, when we die, we live forever in the presence of God Himself. Now *that* is living and we don't know the half of it!

To life! L'Chaim.

Appendix 1:
Recommended Reading

Here are a few books that I think you will find useful, arranged by chapter of this book.

I've heard of this church
The Bible, The Acts of the Apostles, Dr Luke 70 AD (approx)

How the plot was lost
Biblical Church, Beresford Job, Bethany Publishing 2008

No going back?
The Dilemma of Laodicea, Jacob Prasch, Moriel Ministries 2010

The Way revisited
The Pilgrim Church, E. H. Broadbent, Gospel Folio Press, 2009

Home, James!
The Bible, The Letter of James, Ya'acov ben Yosef 50 AD (approx)

The tale of two mindsets
Hebrew thought compared with Greek, Thorleif Boman, W. W. Norton & Co., 2002

A leap in faith
Speak Lord! ... but Who's Listening! Chris Hill, C L Ministries, 2008

Big father
The Truth is Out There, Steve Maltz, Saffron Planet, 2006

Small is dutiful
Our Lost Legacy, John Garr, Golden Keys Books (2001)

Family matters
Our Father Abraham, Marvin Wilson, Eerdmans, 1989

Gimme, gimme!
Rees Howells, Intercessor, Norman Grubb, Lutterworth, 2003

The 64 million dollar question
How the Church lost the Truth, Steve Maltz, Saffron Planet, 2010

Yeshua ben Yosef
Jesus, Man of Many Names, Steve Maltz, Saffron Planet, 2007

A good reflection?
Judaism and Christianity, Trude Weiss-Rosmarin, Jonathan David Publishers 1997

One New Man
How the Church lost the Way, Steve Maltz, Saffron Planet, 2009

Bind us together
The Seduction of Christianity, Hunt & McMahon, Harvest House, 1985

Appendix 2:
Now Why Don't You ... ?

At the current time six of my books are still available for purchase, either through Amazon, Christian bookshops or directly from www.messianicmall.com

How the Church lost The Way...
... and how it can find it again
The story of how the Church has been infiltrated by a pagan virus that has worked its way through every facet of our Christian life and how we can start fighting back.

"With great insight, explaining many concepts simply, Steve Maltz brings us back to the root of our Christian faith. I believe that every pastor and ordinand in the country will benefit from reading this book."

Mark Weeden, Senior Pastor, Worthing Tabernacle

How the Church lost The Truth...
... and how it can find it again
What has happened to some key battlegrounds of Christian Truth and how it is that the Church has managed to lose so much that had been revealed to it in the Bible.

"I really enjoyed reading it. You are the master of epigrams, full of Jewish wit and humour, which I love.

These keep you reading and make the whole interesting. It's
so important to add gravy to the meat and you are a good
chef. I hope this book will reach those who need it most
though I fear they will be irritated, if not infuriated, by
your dismissal of so many of their heroes!"

David Pawson (international Bible teacher)

The Land of Many Names
**Towards a Christian understanding of the Middle East
conflict.**

This book has been generally accepted in the UK as the most
balanced, well-reasoned and clear explanation of the position
taken by those Christians who believe that God still has a purpose
for Israel today.

"This book lives up to the blurb in its style – lively,
entertaining and provocative – it gives a well-researched
and popular account of Israel's history from the days
of Abram to Sharon ... Addictive, dented some of my
convictions and made me think hard"

Tony Sargent,
~ Principal of International Christian College, Glasgow

The People of Many Names
**Towards a clearer understanding of the miracle of the
Jewish people.**

This book pulls no punches in providing an insight into God's
plan for the Jew, Christian antisemitism and includes practical
suggestions for reconciliation within the Body of Messiah.

'I think it's brilliant, inspired, a great read, of interest
to both Jews and Christians, a breath of fresh air – and
timely! What more can I say!'

Julia Fisher, writer and broadcaster.

Jesus, the Man of Many Names

A Fresh Understanding from the dawn of time to the End of Days

Are you prepared for a new book about Jesus that does offer fresh insights without boasting new revelations? Drawing on sources from the Jewish world, ancient and modern, the author will take you on an exhilarating, lively and entertaining exploration of the life and times of the Jewish Messiah.

"Steve Maltz has a gift for combining pacy writing with crystal-clear distillation of his own careful study of scholarly resources and a firm grip on the Gospel. The result is a fascinating new landscape of insight"

David Andrew, editor Sword Magazine

The Truth is out there

The Ultimate World Conspiracy. Who really is pulling the strings?

Is history just a random sequence of events, or are there secret manipulations? What makes us tick? How did the World as we see it come to be? Read this book if you are prepared to be challenged.

Steve Maltz has a rare gift of being able to communicate complex ideas in a way that leaves you thinking that you have read the work of a genius but can still follow his argument clearly. A brilliant read for an evangelist to engage with a sceptic or to give as a gift for "food for thought"

Tim Leffler, The GoodBookstall.org.uk

Appendix 3:
Going Further

This book is really just the beginning of our journey, not the end of it. If you are inspired to go further, here are two possibilities:

SMALL GROUP STUDY GUIDE

There are study notes available to help small groups progress together through the material in this book.

There is more information at www.tolifestudyguide.com

SEMINAR SERIES

Steve and his team will be happy to come to your church to lead a series of seminars over a long weekend, entitled "Church: Lost and Found", based on the material from this book and his previous two books.

This comprises of seven sessions entitled:

How problems in the Early Church still affect us now.

How Plato and Aristotle messed with our minds.

Why the Church needs to look again at its origins.

Living Hebraically – looking at relationships.

Thinking Hebraically – looking at influences.

Acting Hebraically – looking at behaviour.

Summary and Q & A session.

For more information visit www.tolifeseminars.com